God Wants You Healed

by

Al Jennings

All Scripture text is taken from the New King James Version unless otherwise specified with permission granted as stated below:

Scriptures marked NKJV are taken from the NEW KING JAMES VERSION (NKJV): Scripture taken from the NEW KING JAMES VERSION®. Copyright© 1982 by Thomas Nelson, Inc. Used by permission. All rights reserved.

Scriptures marked NIV are taken from the NEW INTERNATIONAL VERSION (NIV): Scripture taken from THE HOLY BIBLE, NEW INTERNATIONAL VERSION ®. Copyright© 1973, 1978, 1984, 2011 by Biblica, Inc.TM. Used by permission of Zondervan.

Scriptures marked TLB are taken from the THE LIVING BIBLE (TLB): Scripture taken from THE LIVING BIBLE copyright© 1971. Used by permission of Tyndale House Publishers, Inc., Carol Stream, Illinois 60188. All rights reserved

Scripture quotations marked "AMP" are taken from the Amplified Bible, Copyright 1954, 1958, 1962, 1964, 1965, 1987 by the Lockman Foundation. Used by permission.

Scripture quotations marked "KJV" are taken from the Holy Bible, King James Version (Public Domain).

Companion Bible. Bullinger. 1901-Haywood. 2005 (Public Domain)

ISBN: 9781691519484

First Printing, 2003 Summit Publications.
Second Printing, 2019 AJ Publishing.

Copyright © 2019, 2003 AJ Publishing. All rights reserved.

Printed in the United States of America. No part of this publication may be reproduced in any form or by any means, including scanning, photocopying, or otherwise without prior written permission of the copyright holder.

Table of Contents

Introduction	1
1. The Origin of Sickness and Disease	3
2. Faith Begins Where the Will of God Is Known	15
3. A Foundation for Healing	25
4. Jesus Was the Will of God in Action	47
5. The Purpose of Preaching and Teaching	59
6. Roadblocks to Healing	67
7. Is God Glorified Through Sickness?	101
8. Redeemed from the Curse of Sickness	113
9. Discerning the Lord's Body	119
10. Dealing with Sickness and Tragedy in the Church	121
11. How to Minister to the Sick Through the Laying on of Hands	129
12. How to Deal with an Attack of Sickness and Disease	139
13. Healing Confessions	145

INTRODUCTION

So many people in the body of Christ do not understand that it is God's will to heal them. Some think that God puts sickness and disease on people to teach them something. Some think healing went out with the last apostle. Others think that He will only heal some, but not all. Still, others think that when you pray for healing, you must close the prayer by saying, 'If it be thy will'.

In this book, I will show you from the Word of God that it is God's will to heal everyone, everywhere and every time. God is looking for people who will dare to believe Him and claim their healing according to the Word of God.

This book is an in-depth study on the subject of healing. I deal with several topics. Including whether God puts sickness on people, the origin of sickness and disease, whether God is glorified through sickness, how to glorify God in our bodies, roadblocks to healing, whether it is God's will to heal everyone, whether sickness is a blessing, what really happened to Job, Paul's thorn, what happened to the blind man in John, Chapter 9, healing in the ministry of Jesus, how healing is received, whether healing went out with the last apostle, whether all healings are instantaneous, whether it is God's will to heal everyone, and why everyone is not healed.

1.
The Origin of Sickness and Disease

Now it came to pass, as Peter went through all parts of the country, that he also came down to the saints who dwelt in Lydda. There he found a certain man named Aeneas, who had been bedridden eight years and was paralyzed. And Peter said to him, "Aeneas, JESUS THE CHRIST HEALS YOU. Arise and make your bed." Then he arose immediately —Acts 9:32-34

Peter knew it was God's will for Aeneas to be well, so he boldly proclaimed it. We need to know today that it is God's will for His people to be well. Healing did not go out with the last apostle; healing goes out when people stop believing for it.

First of all, let us deal with the question, "Where does sickness come from?" Many people think that bad things and catastrophes such as hurricanes, tornadoes, storms, and floods come from God. They think God has some kind of purpose in these things to make us better Christians. But catastrophes, tragedies, sicknesses, and diseases do not come from God. Let me prove this to you from the Word of God.

> Mark 4:36-39
> 36 Now when they had left the multitude they took Him along in the boat as He was. And other little boats were also with Him.
> 37 And a great windstorm arose, and the waves beat into the boat, so that it was already filling.
> 38 But He was in the stern, asleep on a pillow. And they awoke Him and said to Him, "Teacher, do You not care that we are perishing?"
> 39 Then He arose and rebuked the wind, and said to the sea, "PEACE, BE STILL!" And the wind ceased and there was a great calm. (Emphasis added)

The disciples were in the boat when a great windstorm arose. They were troubled by it, but Jesus was asleep in the back of the boat. When they woke Jesus, He rebuked the wind and said to the sea, "Peace, be still!" Verse 39 states that the wind ceased and there was a great calm.

Now according to some people, catastrophes such as this great storm come from God. But that could not be true because Jesus was God manifested in the flesh. Jesus rebuked the wind and calmed the sea. If this storm came from God, then God would be working against Himself, and Jesus would be coming against the will of God. If God had caused this storm, Jesus would not have violated God's will by stopping that storm. This was proof that catastrophes do not come from God.

Where do catastrophes come from? They come from Satan. And yet, some people would have you to believe that these things come from God. In fact, insurance company policies state that catastrophes such as tornadoes, floods, hurricanes, etc., are acts of God. Actually, they are not acts of God at all. They are acts of Satan.

Now, let us specifically look into the area of sickness and disease, and let me prove to you from the Word of God that sickness and disease come from the devil.

> Acts 10:38
> 38 how God anointed Jesus of Narazeth with the Holy Spirit and with power, who went about doing good and healing all WHO WERE OPPRESSED BY THE DEVIL, for God was with Him. (Emphasis added)

Peter is preaching here, and he states, "... God anointed Jesus of Nazareth with the Holy Spirit and with power, who went about doing good and healing all who were oppressed by the devil, for God was with Him."

Peter says Jesus healed, in His earthly ministry, all who were satanically oppressed. Jesus healed all who were oppressed by the devil, not all who were oppressed by God. Now, this shows us that sickness and disease do not come from God; it is satanic oppression.

> Acts 10:38 (NIV)
> 38 how God anointed Jesus of Nazareth with the Holy Spirit and power, and how he went around doing good and healing all who were under the power of the devil, because God was with him.

Sickness and disease are the works of the devil, and Jesus, in His earthly ministry, went about destroying the works of the devil. One of those works was sickness. Jesus was destroying the works of the devil by healing the sick. It is important that we realize where sickness comes from because we do not want anything that comes from the devil. When we know that sickness comes from the devil, then, we will do what we can to resist it. You would not open your mailbox if you thought a bomb was ticking inside. Well, we should treat sickness and disease like a time bomb that the devil is trying to deliver to us. Resist it, in Jesus' name.

God does not put sickness and disease on people. Satan is the author of sickness and disease. But he likes to fool us into believing that God puts sickness on us. He gets multitudes of Christians to blame God for what he does, which is putting sickness and disease on people. Let us look at the following verses.

> Luke 13:10-16
> 10 Now He was teaching in one of the synagogues on the Sabbath.
> 11 And behold, there was a woman who had a spirit of infirmity eighteen years, and was bent over and could in no way raise herself up.
> 12 But when Jesus saw her, He called her to Him and said to her, "Woman, you are loosed from your infirmity."
> 13 And He laid His hands on her, and immediately she was made straight, and glorified God.

> 14 But the ruler of the synagogue answered with indignation, because Jesus had healed on the Sabbath; and he said to the crowd, "There are six days on which men ought to work; therefore come and be healed on them, and not on the Sabbath day."
> 15 The Lord then answered him and said, "Hypocrite! Does not each one of you on the Sabbath loose his ox or donkey from the stall, and lead it away to water it?
> 16 "So ought not this woman, being a daughter of Abraham, WHOM SATAN HAS BOUND—think of it—for eighteen years, be loosed from this bond on the Sabbath?" (Emphasis added)

In verse 16, Jesus says, "So ought not this woman, being a daughter of Abraham, whom Satan has bound—think of it—for eighteen years, be loosed from this bond [or bondage] on the Sabbath?" Here we see that sickness is satanic bondage.

In verse 12 Jesus says, "Woman, you are loosed from your infirmity." He did not say, woman, you are loosed from your blessing from God. Sickness is not a blessing—it is a curse. Jesus says in verse 16, "So ought not this woman...be loosed from this bond [bondage] on the Sabbath." Jesus is saying, in essence, she ought to be loosed.

Jesus reveals who is the author of sickness and disease. He says, "Whom Satan has bound." Sickness and disease are of the devil. We know that sickness and disease are not good because we have doctors who work to rid people of them.

> James 1:17
> 17 EVERY GOOD GIFT AND EVERY PERFECT GIFT IS FROM ABOVE, and comes down from the Father of lights, with whom there is no variation or shadow of turning. (Emphasis added)

James says that every good gift and every perfect gift is from above and comes down from the Father of lights. Every gift that comes from heaven is good. Sickness and disease do not qualify as good gifts. God does not have any sickness and disease to give you. He only has good gifts and good things for His children. Sickness and disease do not come from God—they come from Satan.

Sickness and disease entered into this world because of Adam's sin in the Garden of Eden. Adam was God's first created man. When God put him in the midst of the garden, He told Adam that he may freely eat of every tree in the garden. But of the tree of the knowledge of good and evil he shall not eat, for in the day that he eats of it, he shall surely die (Genesis 2:16,17).

The death that God was referring to was spiritual death. Adam, as we know, ate of the tree of the knowledge of good and evil. Before he ate of that tree, there was no sickness and disease. After he ate of that tree, he died. And we know that the death that he died from was not physical death because he continued living hundreds of years after he ate of the tree. But what God told him was true. The day that he ate of that tree, he died. He was spiritually dead.

Spiritual death is being alienated, cut off, separated, or estranged from God. The moment that Adam ate of that tree, sin entered into the world. Romans 5:12 says, "Therefore, just as through one man sin entered the world, and death through sin, and thus death spread to all men, because all sinned—".

Spiritual death passed on to all men. Why? The reason was because of Adam's sin in the Garden of Eden. Sickness and disease is a by-product of the sin Adam committed in the garden. When Adam ate of that tree, he died instantly, spiritually, and began to die physically. So sickness and disease came into the world as a result of Adam's sin. It is the foul offspring of its mother, sin and its father, Satan. God has nothing to do with sickness and disease. Let us look at healing in the Old Testament.

> Exodus 15:26
> 26 "If you diligently heed the voice of the LORD your God and do what is right in His sight, give ear to His commandments and keep all His statutes, I will put none of the diseases on you which I have brought on

the Egyptians. FOR I AM THE LORD WHO HEALS YOU." (Emphasis added)

It is very significant to note that God establishes Himself as The Healer. The phrase, "For I am the LORD who heals you," means Jehovah Rapha in Hebrew. Jehovah Rapha is one of God's redemptive names, and He reveals Himself in this verse through this name. God's names reveal His character. The Healer is one of His names.

Some people accuse God of putting sickness and disease on them, but that is impossible. God cannot do that because putting sickness on people is not in His character, and there is no sickness in heaven. God does not have any sickness to give you.

Sickness and disease come from all sorts of different places as implied by illnesses such as the Asian Flu and the Hong Kong Flu. But no one has ever heard of the heavenly flu—have you? No, of course not! And the reason for that is because God does not have any sickness.

Since God is the one who is healing you, He cannot be the one who is making you sick, and I will prove it. That is worth repeating. If God is the one who is healing you, He cannot be the one who is making you sick. If He is the one who is healing you and the one who is making you sick, He will not have to heal you if He wants you well. All He has to do is to stop making you sick, and then you will not have any need for healing.

God is Jehovah Rapha, the Lord that heals you. His name is Healer. This reveals to us that it is God's will for His people, His children, to be well.

God Does Not Cause Sickness

Now let us look into an area that trips many people up concerning the subject of healing. When you are reading the Old Testament from the King James Bible translation, it appears as though God (in many cases) puts sickness and disease on people. The scripture we looked at in Exodus 15:26 is one of those examples. God says, "I will put none of the diseases on you which I have brought on the Egyptians."

The Old Testament was originally written in Hebrew, and our modern English Bibles are translations from the original Hebrew. (The New Testament was originally written in Greek.) Now I am not a Hebrew scholar, but Dr. Robert Young, the author of Young's Analytical Concordance, has written a book titled Hints to Bible Interpretation. In this book, he said that the verb in verses such as Exodus 15:26 was written in the permissive sense in the original Hebrew. But because there were no corresponding permissive verbs in the English language, the verbs were translated in the causative sense.

Now before we go any further, I want to make sure you understand what Dr. Young is saying because this will go a long way in your understanding of the Bible. This will help you in studying your Bible and in understanding the character and nature of God. There is a difference between God causing something and God permitting something.

When God said in Exodus 15:26, "I will put none of the diseases on you which I have brought on the Egyptians," it appears as though God was causing the sickness. But in the original Hebrew, the verbs were written in the permissive sense. So actually, it was not God who brought the disease. More accurately, He allowed or permitted the disease.

God did not cause the diseases—He allowed the diseases. Correctly translated, this verse would read something like this, "I will not allow the diseases to come on you that I allowed to come on the Egyptians, for I am the LORD who heals you."

Now that brings us to a statement that many people make: "I know that God does not cause sickness and disease, but God allows it." Well, it is true that God allows it, but not in the way many people think.

Just because God allows things, it does not mean that it is His will. God allows everything that happens. If a person gets raped, robs a bank, or kills someone, God allows it. We know from 2 Corinthians 4:4 that Satan is the god of this world and the bad things that happen in this earth do not come from God—they come from Satan. Sure, God allows it. God allows everything that happens, but that does not mean that it is His will.

The body of Christ has been given authority over all the works of the devil. Jesus says in Matthew 16:19, "And I will give you the keys of the kingdom of heaven, and whatever you bind on earth will be bound in heaven, and whatever you loose on earth will be loosed in heaven."

It is up to us as Christians to bind Satan on the earth. The word bind means to stop or refuse to allow. Satan will control and dominate you if you do not do something about it. Use your authority to bind him and refuse to allow him to control your life. If you do not use your authority, Satan will come in and cause havoc in your life.

Since God did not stop Satan from coming in, people think it must have been God's will for that thing to happen in their life so that they may be perfected. But my friend, God did not hire Satan to perfect the Church. We need to realize that temptations, tests, and trials do not come from God—they come from Satan.

James 1:13 says, "Let no one say when he is tempted, 'I am tempted by God.'" The word tempted means tested or tried. So this verse is saying, "Let no one say when he is tempted, tested or tried, I am tempted, tested, and tried of God, for God cannot be tempted, tested, or tried with evil, neither tempteth, testeth, or trieth He any man."

God is not the author of temptations, tests, and trials. He does not put them on us or allow them to happen to us to teach us something. The purpose of temptations, tests, and trials is to destroy you, and its author is Satan. Now I will say this, if you use the Word in the midst of adverse circumstances, you will come out stronger. God will use the temptations, tests, and trials as stepping stones for your growth and your faith.

Adverse circumstances, contrary to what a lot of people believe, do not really make you strong. It is what you do in the trial that makes you strong. If it is just the temptation that makes you strong, then the people who have had the most tests should be the strongest. But we know that is not true because many people are tested and tried all the time, and they are not any stronger than they were before.

It depends on what you do in the test, the temptation, or the trial that will determine whether you will become stronger. When you use the Word of God against the test, you will always come out on top and become stronger when you come through it. You will always come through it when you use your faith in the trial.

We should not avoid anything that comes from God. If we really believe that sickness comes from God then why do we do whatever we can to get well? Would you prefer not to see a doctor or take medicine because it may take you out of God's will? No, you really desire to get better. If God puts sickness on you to teach you something, then you should not go to the doctor or take medicine. So you see, the whole concept does not make sense.

Here is an example of what people mean when they say, "Well God allowed the tests." Let us say a burglar is breaking into your neighbor's house, and you are watching it from your bedroom window. You see this person attempting to break open the door.

Now you are watching the whole thing, and you can call the police to the scene to prevent the burglary. Instead, you do not do anything; you allow the burglar to break into the house. The burglar has a U-Haul in your neighbor's driveway and proceeds to take out all of the items in the house, and he is in there for a good two hours.

Now what you are doing is watching the whole burglary take place, and you are not doing a thing about it. So what have you done? You have allowed that burglar to rob your neighbor and take away everything that he has.

This is what many people think God does. He watches or allows the devil to cause trouble in their lives. Despite God's ability to stop it, He does not. Since God did not intervene when they were in trouble, they think it must have happened for a reason. Does everything happen for a reason? Yes, but the reason why trouble comes to many Christians is because they do not take authority over the enemy. Sadly, many Christians do not realize they have authority over the devil.

When the devil does come in to steal from us (for his purpose is to steal, to kill, and to destroy —John 10:10), and we do not rise up and use our authority to stop it from happening, God watches it happen. He has the ability to stop it from happening, but He cannot stop it from happening.

The reason why God cannot stop it is because we do not give Him permission to get involved. We do not exercise our authority. If you do not bind on earth as Jesus said in Matthew 16:19, then it will not be bound in heaven. "Whatever you bind on earth will be bound in heaven, and whatever you loose on earth will be loosed in heaven." If you do not bind on earth, it "won't be" bound in heaven. If you do not loose on earth, it "won't be" loosed in heaven.

God does not want the devil to walk on Christians. In fact, in Luke 10:19 it says, "Behold, I give you the authority to trample on serpents and scorpions, and over all the power of the enemy, and nothing shall by any means hurt you." You see, it is God's will for you to walk on the devil, not for him to walk on you. God does not want the devil to control you or to mess over you. Yes, God allows everything but that does not mean it is His will for it to happen.

Whatever Satan does to you, it is not God's will for it to happen. It is not that God does not want to do anything about it, it is because you allow it to happen. You allow Satan to get a foothold. The Bible tells us in Ephesians 4:27, "nor give place to the devil." Do not give him any ground to step on.

Suppose it was pouring rain and your child had to walk to school. You would tell your child to put on a raincoat and take an umbrella. If the child refuses to obey you and goes outside without the umbrella and the raincoat, your child would get drenched in the rain and arrive at school soaking wet. That child cannot say to you, "You made me get wet." No, what you did was to provide the child the means whereby he could stay dry. But if the child refuses to take advantage of the tools you give him, he will pay a penalty for it.

That is the same thing that happens to us as children of God. If we do not use the faith, the authority, and the armor of God that has been given to us, the devil can take advantage of us. Is it God's will? NO! It is your refusal to walk in your covenant privileges and your refusal to use the resources that God has provided for your victory that allows the devil to walk over you.

Here are some examples of verbs being translated in the causative sense when, originally, they were written in the permissive sense.

> Isaiah 45:7
> 7 "I form the light and create darkness, I make peace
> and create calamity; I, the LORD, do all these things."

It says here that, "I [God] form the light and create darkness." God does form light, but He does not create darkness. First John 1:5 says,

"God is light and in Him is no darkness at all." So God cannot create darkness because He does not have any.

Isaiah 45:7 goes on to say, "I make peace and create calamity; I, the LORD, do all these things." Well, God does make peace, but He does not create calamity. This is an example of verbs that were translated in the causative sense rather than in the permissive sense. It should have been translated as, "I form the light and allow darkness, I make peace and allow calamity; I, the LORD, do all these things."

> Amos 3:6 (KJV)
> 6 Shall a trumpet be blown in the city, and the people not be afraid? Shall there be evil in a city, and the LORD hath not done it?

If you take this verse at face value, it looks like the Lord causes evil. Now certainly, the Lord is not the author of evil, and the Lord is not the author of calamity. This verse should have been translated as, "If there is calamity in a city, will not the Lord have allowed it?" Let us look at another verse.

> 1 Samuel 16:14 (KJV)
> 14 But the Spirit of the LORD departed from Saul, and an evil spirit from the LORD troubled him.

The verse says, "The Spirit of the LORD departed from Saul and an evil spirit [some translations say a distressing spirit] from the LORD troubled him." Now if you look at it this way, it gives you the idea that the Lord had sent an evil spirit to trouble Saul. But God does not have evil spirits to send to people. Evil spirits come from Satan. What actually happened was that the Lord allowed the evil spirit or distressing spirit to trouble Saul.

You see, God allows evil, calamity, and destruction. He cannot help but allow it because we as humans are free moral agents. If we do not operate in line with God's laws, precepts, and principles, and thus violate them, we open the door for Satan to enter in and cause evil, destruction, and calamity. There is nothing God can do about it. He has to allow it because we allow it.

It is not God who steals, kills and destroys. It is Satan because the Bible says in 2 Corinthians 4:4 that he's the god of this world. Satan has a right to be here until Jesus comes back and evicts him from the earth. But until then, he will be here to come against the Christian as the antagonist of the children of God.

First Peter 5:8 says, "The devil walks about like a roaring lion, seeking whom he may devour." That tells us that he does not have to devour us, but he seeks those whom he may devour. Christians, who do not use their God-given authority to put the devil in his place, allow him to devour them. I want to remind you that, according to Luke 10:19, we have been given the authority to "trample on serpents and scorpions, and over all the power of the enemy." The Bible says, "Nothing shall by any means hurt you."

2.
Faith Begins Where the Will of God Is Known

So then faith comes by hearing, and hearing by the word of God.
—Romans 10:17

Now the parable is this: The SEED is the word of God. —Luke 8:11

God's Word is the seed with which we are to plant in our hearts. For us to receive healing from God, we have to exercise faith or appropriate faith for our healing. Faith begins where the will of God is known. Until we know what is God's will, there is nothing on which to base our faith.

Appropriating faith cannot go beyond one's actual knowledge of the revealed will of God. God's Word is the seed. It is the Word of God planted, watered, and steadfastly trusted that heals the body. The seed must remain planted and kept watered before it can produce its harvest.

Let me give you an example. Let us say I am speaking to a large congregation of 100,000 people, and one of them is a billionaire. Let us establish the fact that he has one billion dollars that he can give away. Let us say He announces after service that he is going to give two people $10,000 each.

If you were sitting in that congregation of 100,000 people, would you have faith to believe that you would be one of the two to receive $10,000? Well, you really cannot exercise any faith for that since you do not know whether you are one of the two who will receive $10,000.

Let us say, on the other hand, this same billionaire announces that he is going to give everyone—all 100,000 in the congregation—$10,000 each after service. Now, where is your faith level? Do you have faith to believe that you will receive $10,000? Well, all things being equal and assuming that this billionaire is a man of his word, you have sufficient grounds for faith because you know his will is to give everyone $10,000. Since you are one of the 100,000, you can have faith to believe you will receive $10,000.

Now let us take this illustration over to the area of healing. For you to really base your faith on God's Word that it is His will to heal you, you must know that it is His will to heal all and not some.

If you believe that it is God's will to heal only some and not all, you do not have sufficient grounds for faith. You do not have anything upon which to base your faith. You cannot appropriate faith for your healing. If that is what you believe, you will not know for sure if you are one of the ones that God wants to heal.

On the other hand, if you believe according to God's Word that it is His will to heal everybody (His will is His Word), you have sufficient grounds to release your faith. Now you know that you are, indeed, one of the ones for whom it is His will to heal.

Faith begins where the will of God is known. If you can just renew your mind to the fact that it is absolutely God's will to heal everybody, you will know that it is His will to heal you too since you are included in everybody. You can release your faith. You can appropriate faith for healing because you know it is God's will to heal you.

It is so important that we get you to a place where you understand that it is God's will to heal you—not the person next door, the usher board member, or the choir member. It is God's will to heal them too, but I want to talk to you right now. I want you to understand that it is God's will to heal YOU!

Now you have to get away from this thinking, this mentality, that it is God's will to heal only some. If that is what you believe, you will be like the person who is sitting in the congregation wondering whether they are going to receive $10,000. In a congregation of 100,000 people, you do not really know if you will be one of the two to receive $10,000. You really do not have grounds for faith to receive $10,000.

That is exactly the same thing that happens with people who need healing. They are hindered from receiving their healing because they are not sure whether it is God's will to heal them.

It Is Not Enough to Know That God Is Able

In this teaching, we are going to show you positive proof from God's Word that it is absolutely His will to heal everybody. In Mark 1:40, a leper came to Jesus and did not know whether it was God's will to heal him. He knew that Jesus was able to heal, but he did not know whether or not He would be willing. God is able, and He has the ability to heal. But it is not enough to know that God is able, we must know that He is willing.

> Mark 1:40-42
> 40 Now a leper came to Him, imploring Him, kneeling down to Him and saying to Him, "If You are willing, You can make me clean."
> 41 Then Jesus, moved with compassion stretched out His hand and touched him, and said to him, "I am willing; be cleansed."
> 42 As soon as He had spoken, immediately the leprosy left him, and he was cleansed.

A leper came to Jesus seeking healing and said, "If You are willing, You can make me clean," or we can say, "If it be Your will, You can make me clean." Now this leper acknowledged the fact that God had the ability to heal him. He did not have a problem with God's ability or whether He could do it. He knew Jesus was able to heal him. His problem, like many Christians today, was that he did not know whether God was willing to heal him.

Verse 41 says that Jesus was moved with compassion. Jesus healed the leper and is still healing the sick today out of His compassion. He answered the man's question and removed the leper's doubt concerning His willingness to heal him. Jesus removed the leper's uncertainty and doubt by saying, "I am willing; be cleansed."

Jesus is the will of God in action. Jesus said He only did what He saw the Father do. We do not ever see Jesus putting sickness on people because the Father does not put sickness on people. And we never see Jesus turning anybody away who came to Him for healing because it has always been God's will for people to be well.

The next verse is very important. It says, "As soon as He had spoken, immediately the leprosy left him, and he was cleansed." What did Jesus speak? What did He say? He said, "I am willing." Jesus was moved with compassion and touched the leper, but nothing happened. Even though Jesus Christ was anointed with the Holy Spirit and power flowed out of Him, nothing happened when He touched the man.

We need to realize that in most cases, Jesus' ministry required faith to rise in the individual. You need to understand that it is not God's power that gets you healed. Now listen to me and do not misunderstand what I am saying. Ultimately, it is God's power that heals you; but it is really not His power that gets you healed.

The proof of that is the fact that God's power is the same all the time. God's power is available to the sick right now, yet some people are healed and other people not. That does not mean that God is unwilling to heal all. It simply means that some people tap into the power that is available and others do not. Anybody can tap into the power of God by faith in God's Word and receive their healing any time they choose. All you have to do is to act on the Word and receive your healing which has already been provided for you.

Jesus was saturated with power. Yet, when He touched the man, nothing happened until He said something. What He said was, "I am willing." As soon as Jesus said that, the man had faith to be healed. The man received his healing, but not by the power of God. Now do not get me wrong. It was the power of God that healed him, but the power of God is available 24 hours a day. The leper received his healing by releasing his faith and, therefore, tapping into God's power.

The same was true in Mark, Chapter 5, with the woman who had the issue of blood. There were all kinds of people surrounding Jesus, and she pressed through the crowd and touched Jesus. Power flowed out of Him and into her body and healed her. Jesus looked around and asked His disciples, "Who touched Me?" And the disciples said, "You see the multitude thronging You, and You say, 'Who touched Me?" I can imagine the disciples saying, "We are doing everything we can to keep all these people off of you, and you are asking us who touched YOU! All kinds of people are touching you."

Jesus realized that someone had touched Him with a different touch. Somebody touched Him with a touch of faith. Many people were touching Jesus, but they did not touch Him with a touch of faith. They did not tap into the power. I am sure there were other people around that were sick; and yet that power, although it was available for them, did not heal them. They did not tap into it as this woman did.

As soon as Jesus spoke the Word and removed the leper's doubt concerning His willingness to heal Him—as soon as this man realized that Jesus was willing to heal him—he received his healing. Mark 1:42 says, "As soon as He had spoken," not as soon as Jesus laid His hands on him. Jesus laid His hands on him and nothing happened until He spoke. And as soon as He said, "I am willing; be cleansed," the leprosy left him. The leper was cleansed.

When the leper knew that God was able to heal him but was uncertain as to whether it was His will to heal him, that was not sufficient grounds for faith. Faith cannot be based on God's ability alone. Faith must be based on God's ability and His willingness. Until you know what God's will is concerning your healing, there is nothing to base your faith on.

We see a similar situation in Luke 5:17. Healing power was available to the Pharisees and teachers of the law, but none of them tapped into it. But some men of faith got up on the roof so that their friend could tap into it.

To know that God is able to heal you but not knowing that He is willing to heal you is like having a seed but not planting it. When you know that God is willing, the seed of the Word is planted.

God's will concerning healing is revealed to us in Isaiah 53:4, "Surely He has borne our griefs (sicknesses)"; Matthew 8:17, "He Himself...bore our sicknesses"; and 1Peter 2:24, "By whose stripes you were healed." These passages clearly reveal God's willingness to heal us. We will go into more detail with these verses later in this book. But I want to give you these passages here in discussing God's willingness and God's will for us to be healed.

Praying If It Be Thy Will Does Not Work for Healing

According to James 5:15, it is the prayer of faith that saves the sick. Too many people pray if it be Thy will concerning their healing such as, "Lord, if it be thy will, heal brother John," or, "If it be Thy will, heal me." Using if it be Thy will when praying for healing is a faith destroying prayer. A prayer of if it be Thy will cannot save the sick because it is a prayer of doubt. If is the badge of doubt. When you say if it be Thy will, you are saying you do not know whether it is His will to heal you.

We know it is God's will to heal based on Isaiah 53:4, Matthew 8:17, and 1 Peter 2:24. So when you say if it be Thy will, you are saying you do not know His will, and you are not sure of His will concerning healing. As a result, you will not receive healing praying that way.

> James 1:6, 7
> 6 But let him ask in faith, with no doubting, for he who doubts is like a wave of the sea driven and tossed by the wind.
> 7 For let not that man suppose that he will receive anything from the Lord;

James says, "He who doubts [a doubting person is one that wavers] is like a wave of the sea driven and tossed by the wind. For let not that man suppose that he will receive anything from the Lord."

James is saying here that if you pray a prayer of doubt such as if it be Thy will, you should not expect to receive anything from the Lord. God wants us to expect to receive healing because it is His will. His will is revealed to us in His Word. When we pray a prayer of faith based on God's willingness to heal us, we will get the results—the results of our healing manifested in our bodies.

Remember, we said earlier that knowing God's willingness to heal us is the planting of the seed. The seed is the Word of God. Praying for healing with the faith destroying words of if it be Thy will is not planting the seed—it is destroying the seed.

"He Himself...bore our sicknesses." Matthew 8:17 is a fulfillment of the prophecy by the Holy Spirit through the Prophet Isaiah in Isaiah

53:4. This reveals to us that Jesus bore our sicknesses at Calvary on the tree (or the cross). First Peter 2:24 tells us that Jesus bore our sins in His own body on the tree. So at Calvary, Jesus bore our sins as well as our sicknesses.

Healing Is Part of the Gospel

The gospel does not leave a man in uncertainty concerning God's will. It tells him what God's will is. The Holy Spirit's words, "He Himself bore our sicknesses" (Matthew 8:17), are as much as a part of the gospel as His words, "Who Himself bore our sins in His own body on the tree" (1 Peter 2:24). I want to show you that healing is part and parcel of the gospel. Many people do not realize that healing is a very important part of the gospel.

We need to realize that Jesus spent more time in His ministry healing than He did doing any other thing. And I am here to tell you that Jesus is still healing the sick today. He has not gone out of the healing business. He has not turned over healing to the Surgeon General (doctors).

I appreciate doctors and everything that they can do. I want to go on record as saying that I am not against doctors. Thank God for them. But what we are talking about here is divine healing, and God is still healing the sick today by His Word and His Spirit.

Jesus says in John 14:12, "He who believes in Me, the works that I do he will do also; and greater works than these he will do." That is a very astounding statement because Jesus says, "The works that I do you will do also." So we can do the works of Jesus, and healing was one of the works of Jesus.

The works of Jesus consisted of teaching, preaching, and healing. We will look into the importance of teaching a little later in this book because there is a connection between the teaching of the Word and healing. Teaching, preaching, and healing goes hand-in-hand.

Jesus is still healing the sick today through His Body. In Mark 16:17 and 18, He says, "And these signs will follow those who believe...they will lay hands on the sick, and they will recover."

Luke, the writer of Acts, says in Acts 1:1, "The former account [which was the gospel of Luke] I made, O Theophilus, of all that Jesus began both to do and teach." Notice Luke says, "...all that Jesus began both to do and teach." So Luke summarizes the ministry of Jesus as all that He began to do.

What Jesus began to do, obviously, He has not finished doing. He began His healing ministry, and He continues His healing ministry at the right hand of the Father through the Body of Christ—the Church. Jesus says, "The works that I do he [you] will do also; and greater works than these he [you] will do, because I go to My Father."

> Acts 14:7-10
> 7 And they were preaching the gospel there.
> 8 And in Lystra a certain man without strength in his feet was sitting, a cripple from his mother's womb, who had never walked.
> 9 This man heard Paul speaking. Paul, observing him intently and seeing that he had faith to be healed,
> 10 said with a loud voice, "Stand up straight on your feet!" And he leaped and walked.

In verse 7, we find that Paul was preaching the gospel. Verse 8 says there was a man in Lystra who was a cripple from birth. He had never walked. Now verse 9 says the man heard Paul speak. What was Paul speaking about? Verse 7 says he preached the gospel. So the man heard Paul preach the gospel, and Paul observed him intently and saw that he had faith to be healed.

Romans 10:17 says, "So then faith comes by hearing, and hearing by the Word of God." To have faith for something, you have to hear the Word on it because faith comes by hearing the Word. Faith is a by-product of the Word of God.

"But what does it say? 'The word is near you, in your mouth and in your heart' (that is, the word of faith which we preach)" (Romans 10:8). The Word of God is called the Word of Faith. Why? Because when the Word is preached, it produces faith in the hearts of the hearers. The Word of God produces faith. You cannot have faith without it. When Romans 10:17 says faith comes, it is obvious that faith is not already there because if faith were already there, it would not have to come. So faith comes by something. It comes by the Word of God. Faith and the Word are like the wet with the water.

When you are in a restaurant, you do not ask the waiter for a glass of water and tell him to make sure that it is wet. When you have the water, you have the wet. When you have the Word, you have faith. This cripple could only have faith by hearing the Word on healing.

For this cripple to have faith to be healed, he must have heard that he could be healed or that God wanted him well. The only way he could have faith for healing is by hearing the Word on healing.

Notice these verses did not say that Paul preached healing—it only says that he preached the gospel. So if you just use some spiritual, deductive reasoning, you can see very clearly that healing must be a part of the gospel. Otherwise, how does this guy, who was crippled from birth, get the idea that he can be healed when all he heard Paul preach was the gospel? If the gospel consisted only of salvation from sin, then this guy would not have had any faith to be healed because he would not have heard anything about healing.

Think about it for a moment. The man was just sitting there crippled as he has always been, minding his own business. Paul comes around and starts preaching the gospel and, all of a sudden, he gets this bright idea that he can be healed. It says here that Paul perceived that this man had faith to be healed.

The only way to have faith for something, according to Romans 10:17 is by hearing the Word. So when Paul preached the gospel, he preached the full gospel, which included healing. And the man, a cripple from birth, heard that God wanted him well. I believe Paul preached that Jesus took our sins and sicknesses at Calvary. Jesus bore our sins and our sicknesses so that we can be free of sin and sickness.

The crippled man heard that and faith rose up in him to be healed. When Paul perceived that this man had faith to be healed, Acts 14:10 states, "[Paul] said with a loud voice, 'Stand up straight on your feet!' And he leaped and walked." This all happened because Paul preached the gospel which included healing. Healing is part and parcel of the gospel.

Romans 1:16
16 For I am not ashamed of the gospel of Christ, for it is the power of God to salvation for everyone who believes, for the Jew first and also for the Greek.

Paul says here that the gospel is the power of God unto salvation. Salvation is an all-inclusive word, which includes healing. It also means preservation, safety, soundness, and deliverance. So we can say the gospel is the power of God unto preservation. The gospel is the power of God unto safety. The gospel is the power of God unto soundness. The gospel is the power of God unto deliverance. The gospel is the power of God unto healing. Healing refers to salvation in the physical sense.

3.
A Foundation for Healing

However the report went around concerning Him all the more; and great multitudes came together to HEAR, AND TO BE HEALED by Him of their infirmities. —Luke 5:15 (Emphasis Added)

And He came down with them and stood on a level place with a crowd of His disciples and a great multitude of people from all Judea and Jerusalem, and from the seacoast of Tyre and Sidon, who came to HEAR HIM AND BE HEALED of their diseases, —Luke 6:17 (Emphasis Added)

It is important for people who desire to be healed to first hear the Word of God on the subject of healing. They need to get a foundation of the Word concerning healing established for themselves in their spirit. I think many times we pray too quickly for someone's healing. People need to spend time hearing the Word on healing before they are actually prayed for.

These verses reveal to us that in Jesus' ministry, people came to hear Him and to be healed. Notice the hearing came before the healing. They came to listen to Him teach, and they were healed. I realize in some situations you may need to pray immediately, but if at all possible, instead of saying, "Pray for me," people should first say, "Teach me God's Word so that I can intelligently cooperate for my recovery." The prayer of faith (which is to heal the sick) is to follow, not proceed the planting of the "seed" (the Word) upon which alone faith is based.

Exodus 23:25

25 "So you shall serve the LORD your God, and He will bless your bread and your water. And I will take sickness away from the midst of you."

God was Israel's Healer under the Old Covenant. So as long as they walked in obedience to the terms of that covenant, they lived in divine health. Here God says He will take sickness out of their midst. If sickness is taken out of your midst, you do not have to put up with it. Isaiah 53:3 thru 6 reveals to us our healing redemption.

Jesus Took Our Sicknesses on the Cross

Isaiah 53:3-6

3 He is despised and rejected by men, A Man of sorrows and acquainted with grief. And we hid, as it were, our faces from Him; He was despised, and we did not esteem Him.
4 Surely He has borne our griefs And carried our sorrows; Yet we esteemed Him stricken, smitten by God, and afflicted.
5 But He was wounded for our transgressions, He was bruised for our iniquities; The chastisement for our peace was upon Him, And by His stripes we are healed.
6 All we like sheep have gone astray; We have turned, every one, to his own way; And the LORD has laid on Him the iniquity of us all.

Isaiah 53:10-12

10 Yet it pleased the LORD to bruise Him; He has put Him to grief.
When You make His soul an offering for sin, He shall see His seed, He shall prolong His days, And the pleasure of the LORD shall prosper in His hand.

A Foundation for Healing

11 He shall see the labor of His soul, and be satisfied. By His knowledge My righteous servant shall justify many, for He shall bear their iniquities.
12 Therefore I will divide Him a portion with the great, and He shall divide the spoil with the strong, Because He poured out His soul unto death, and He was numbered with the transgressors, and He bore the sin of many, and made intercession for the transgressors.

In Isaiah 53:4, there is a footnote in my Bible by the words *griefs* and *sorrows*. The footnote states that the word *griefs* in the Hebrew literally mean sickness, and the word *sorrows* in the Hebrew mean pains. Unfortunately, the translators misinterpreted griefs and sorrows because, originally, these words actually meant sickness and pains.

In verse 3 it says that Jesus was a man of sorrows and acquainted with grief. Again, there is a footnote by the words *sorrows* and *griefs*. The word *sorrows* literally mean pains, and the word *griefs* are interpreted as sickness. So what is actually being said is the following:

> He is despised and rejected by men [this is a prophecy concerning the Lord Jesus Christ at Calvary's cross], A Man of PAINS and acquainted with SICKNESS. And we hid, as it were, our faces from Him; He was despised, and we did not esteem Him. Surely He has borne our SICKNESSES and carried our PAINS; Yet we esteemed Him stricken, Smitten by God, and afflicted. But He was wounded for our transgressions, He was bruised for our iniquities; The chastisement for our peace was upon Him, And by His stripes we are healed.
> —Isaiah 53:3-5 (Emphasis Added)

The reason it states "by His stripes we are healed" is because Jesus bore our sicknesses and carried our pains. In Isaiah, Chapter 53, lies the key to the subject of healing. There are two words translated here in Isaiah 53:4 as griefs and sorrows. The word *griefs* are the Hebrew word *choli*, and the word *sorrows* are the Hebrew word *makob*. These words have been incorrectly translated as griefs and sorrows.

These two Hebrew words mean sicknesses and pains throughout the Old Testament. The word *choli* is interpreted as disease or sickness in the following scriptures: Deuteronomy 7:15, Deuteronomy 28:59, 1 Kings 17:17, 2 Kings 1:2, 2 Kings 8:8-9, 2 Chronicles 16:12, and 2 Chronicles 21:15, 18, 19. The word *makob* is interpreted as pain in Job 14:22 and Job 33:19. This supports the reason why verse 4 should be stated as "Surely He has borne our sicknesses and carried our pains."

Now let us read the 53rd Chapter of Isaiah from other translations. But before we do that, let me prove to you again that these two words in question were incorrectly translated. I want to prove this to you because it is very vital for you to understand that Jesus Christ at Calvary actually took away your sins as well as your sicknesses and pains. The best evidence that these words were mistranslated is found in the Holy Spirit's own words in Matthew 8:17. The best way to understand the Bible is to let scripture interpret scripture.

Matthew 8:17 is a direct quotation from Isaiah 53:4. We can see here how the Holy Spirit translated Isaiah 53:4. It is interesting and very revealing to see that the Holy Spirit does not use the words *griefs* and *sorrows*. It says in Matthew 8:16, "When evening had come, they brought to Him many who were demon-possessed. And He cast out the spirits with a word, and healed all who were sick," Notice in verse 17 it says, "That it might be fulfilled which was spoken by Isaiah the prophet, saying: 'He Himself took our infirmities and bore our sicknesses.'"

Isaiah 53:4 says, "Surely He has borne our griefs." But the Holy Spirit says in Matthew 8:17, "He Himself...bore our sicknesses." That is a direct quotation from Isaiah 53:4, and the Holy Spirit uses the word *sicknesses* rather than griefs. So this is evidence that Isaiah 53:4 is telling us that Jesus at Calvary took our sicknesses and carried our pains.

When Jesus said, "It is finished (John 19:30)," all our sins: past, present, and future were forgiven. Now many understand (because we had heard it preached over and over again) that Jesus Christ at Calvary took our sins as a substitutionary sacrifice for sin so that we would not have to bear it. To receive for ourselves what Jesus has done for us at Calvary, all we have to do is to accept Jesus as our personal Savior and Lord. Jesus took our sins at Calvary so that we would not have to.

I want you to understand that at the same time that He took our sins, He also took your sicknesses. Jesus' finished work also provided healing for us. The reason so many people are sick in the body of Christ is because they have never heard this preached or taught.

Romans 10:17 says, "So then faith comes by hearing, and hearing by the word of God." The reason why many people have faith for salvation from sin is because they have heard it preached so much over the years that they can come and receive the free gift of eternal life. The way you receive salvation is the same way you can receive healing.

Many people have the idea that since there are sick Christians in the body of Christ, it must not be God's will to heal everyone. Let us say you have a church service and an invitation is given for people to come to receive Jesus. Some people will come and accept Jesus, but then others will go home without receiving Him. Are you saying then that it was not God's will to save the people who remained unsaved? Are you going to say that it was God's will to save only those who came up to receive their salvation? No, of course not!

You must understand that even though Jesus Christ paid the penalty for the sin of mankind at Calvary, each individual must decide for themselves to believe what Jesus did for them and to receive Him. "If you confess with your mouth the Lord Jesus and believe in your heart that God has raised Him from the dead, you will be saved" (Romans. 10:9).

So if a person refuses to accept Jesus, it is not a matter of whether or not it is God's will for them to be saved. We already know from the Bible that God is "not willing that any should perish but that all should come to repentance" (2 Peter 3:9). Well, the same thing is true concerning healing. The fact that there are sick people in the body of Christ does not mean that God is not willing to heal everybody. It simply means that they have not believed and received their healing for themselves.

We are teaching this to help you to understand these truths so that you know what the Word says on the subject of healing. If we can ever get people to understand that at the same time Jesus took our sins, He also took our sicknesses, it will be easier for them to receive their healing. They will be able to recognize that Jesus was not only their substitutionary sacrifice for their sins, He was also their substitutionary sacrifice for their sicknesses.

Now let us read Dr. Robert Young's translation of the 53rd Chapter of Isaiah, verses 3 thru 6 and verses 10 and 12.

> Isaiah 53:3-6, 10, 12 (Dr. Robert Young)
> 3 He is despised, and left of men, A man of pains [makob], and acquainted with sickness [choli]. And as one hiding the face from us, He is despised, and we esteemed him not.
> 4 Surely our sicknesses [choli] he hath borne, And our pains [makob]—he hath carried them, And we—we have esteemed him plagued, Smitten of God, and afflicted.
> 5 And he is pierced for our transgressions, Bruised for our iniquities, The chastisement of our peace is on him, And by his bruise there is healing to us.
> 6 All of us like sheep have wandered, Each to his own way we have turned, And Jehovah hath caused to meet on him, The punishment of us all.
> 10 And Jehovah hath delighted to bruise him, He hath made him sick [choli], If his soul doth make an offering for guilt, He seeth seed—he prolongeth days,And the pleasure of Jehovah in his hand doth prosper.
> 12...And with transgressors he was numbered, And he the sin of many hath borne, And for transgressors he intercedeth.

Now let us read from Dr. Isaac Lesser's translation of Isaiah 53:3-5 and 10.

A Foundation for Healing

> Isaiah 53:3-5, 10 (Dr. Isaac Lesser)
> 3 He was despised and shunned by men: A man of pains, and acquainted with disease...
> 4 But only our diseases did he bare himself, And our pains he carried...
> 5 And through his bruises was healing granted to us...
> 10 But the Lord was pleased to crush him through disease...

Here is Rotherham's translation of verse 10: "He laid on him sickness." You see healing is a fact and is a forever settled subject as far as heaven is concerned. Healing belongs to you, and you can receive it today by believing and acting on God's Word.

> Isaiah 53:4
> 4 Surely He has borne our griefs And carried our sorrows; Yet we esteemed Him stricken, Smitten by God, and afflicted.

Further proof that Jesus took your sicknesses at Calvary is the fact that the words *borne* and *carried* in verse 4 (concerning the bearing and carrying of our sicknesses and pains) are the same words used to describe Christ bearing our sins. If you study these Hebrews words, you will find that the words *borne* and *carried* refer to the scapegoat in the Old Testament that bear away the sins of the people. The word *bear* in the Hebrew is *nasa* and the word *carried* is *cabal* in the Hebrew. Let us do a word study on these words.

> Leviticus 16:22
> 22 "The goat shall bear [nasa] on itself all their iniquities to an uninhabited land; and he shall release the goat in the wilderness."

Borne (nasa) means to lift up, to bear away, to convey, to remove to a distance, to carry off, to sweep away, or to take away. Carried (cabal) means to carry, to be burdensome, or to bear a load. The very same words, *nasa* and *cabal* (used in verses 11 and 12 to describe the bearing and carrying of our sin) are used in verse 4 to describe the bearing of our sicknesses. Both words signify an assumption of a heavy burden, a substitution (on our behalf), and a completion of removing the thing borne. When Jesus bore and carried away our sins, He also bore and carried away our sicknesses and pains. He actually bore or removed them away!

Jesus bore your sins and sicknesses away to the cross. Sin and sickness have been (past tense) passed from mankind to Calvary. Salvation and divine health have been passed from Calvary to mankind.

Do Not Forget God's Benefit of Healing

> Psalm 103:1-3
> 1 Bless the LORD, O my soul; And all that is within me, bless His holy name!
> 2 Bless the LORD, O my soul, And forget not all His benefits:
> 3 Who forgives all your iniquities, Who heals all your diseases

David says, "Bless the LORD, O my soul; And all that is within me, bless His holy name! Bless the LORD, O my soul, And forget not all His benefits." We are told here that God has benefits for us and available to us, and we are not to forget them. One of His benefits is healing. It says, "Who forgives all your iniquities [sins]." But it does not stop here. It goes on to say, "Who heals all your diseases." Healing is one of the benefits of redemption.

Notice how healing is mentioned right along with the forgiveness of sins as it is in Isaiah, Chapter 53. This tells us that He forgave all our sins or iniquities, and He also healed all of our diseases.

No one will argue with the fact that we have been forgiven of all our sins. When we accept Jesus Christ as our personal Lord and

Savior, we are born again. Our sin is totally wiped away. Our past has been removed, and every single sin that we committed has been blotted out. Well, just as all of our sins are forgiven, all of our diseases are removed because it says, "Who heals all your diseases" (Psalm 103:3).

You Are Healed by Jesus Stripes

We need to realize that healing is a fact and is forever settled in heaven. We received healing of all of our diseases at the same time that we received forgiveness of all our sins at Calvary's cross. So our healing was taken care of nearly 2000 years ago. So as far as God is concerned, you are already healed!

> 1 Peter 2:24
> 24 who Himself bore our sins in His own body on the tree, that we, having died to sins, might live for righteousness—BY WHOSE STRIPES YOU WERE HEALED. (Emphasis added)

Peter said, "Who Himself [Jesus] bore our sins in His own body on the tree [Calvary], that we, having died to sins, might live for righteousness—by whose stripes you were healed." The bearing of our sickness is mentioned right along with the bearing of our sins at Calvary. Jesus died a substitutionary death at Calvary. At the same time that He bore your sins, He bore your sicknesses.

Peter puts it this way, "By whose stripes you were healed." Notice the words *were healed*. Now there is a quotation from Isaiah 53:5 where it says, "And by His stripes we are healed." Isaiah was prophesying into the future when Jesus would one day die at Calvary. But Peter was on the New Covenant side of Calvary, which is the side of Calvary after Jesus' death, burial, and resurrection. Looking back at what Jesus bore at Calvary, Peter says, "You were [past tense] healed." You see, child of God, you were healed. And if you were healed then you are healed, and if you are healed then "you is" healed. Praise the Lord!

What does it mean when it says, "By whose stripes you were healed"? When they took Jesus to the cross, they examined Him—by scourging. In other words, Jesus was beaten with a whip called the cat-o'-nine-tails. This was a leather whip that had nine strands attached to it, and on the end of each strand was a metal bit. Jesus was beaten with thirty-nine stripes. With each lash of the whip, the metal bits would go into His body and pull out chunks of skin. And with every lash of the whip, symbolically, God saw every sickness, every disease, and every pain transferred from mankind to the body of Jesus.

When they took Jesus to the cross and killed Him, they also killed sickness and disease. In other words, they killed the right of sickness and disease to come upon you. Therefore, that explains what "by whose stripes you were healed" really means. Jesus removed, carried away our sickness and diseases.

Now let us go back to Isaiah, Chapter 53, and point out something else in this great redemptive chapter which proves that healing belongs to us today. Looking at verse 6 from Rotherham's translation, the last part of it states, "And Jehovah hath caused to meet on Him the punishment of us all." This means that God has put the punishment of us all on Jesus at Calvary. Now let me ask you this: what was the punishment for our sin? There are several punishments of sin such as separation from God (or spiritual death), condemnation, poverty, mental anxiety, sickness, and disease.

Now we know that separation from God was one of the punishments of sin, and we accept the fact that our sin was laid upon Jesus. Because of that, we are free from sin, and we are no longer separated or alienated from God. Instead, we enjoy communion and fellowship with our heavenly Father because Jesus bore our sin.

There are also other punishments of sin involved, including sickness and disease. Since sickness and disease are among the punishments of sin, then sickness and disease were also laid on Jesus so that we can enjoy divine health. Jesus took the punishment—sin, sickness, and disease, etc.—of us all as our substitute at Calvary so that we would not have to bear it ourselves.

Remember 2 Corinthians 5:21 says, "For He made Him who knew no sin to be sin for us, that we might become the righteousness of God in Him." Everything that Jesus did at Calvary was done for us—none of it was for Himself. You see He was made to be sin. He did not commit any acts of sin, but He was made to be sin who knew no sin. Likewise, He knew no sickness, but He was made to be sickness because Matthew 8:17 says, "He Himself...bore our sicknesses."

When you look at it in this light, we really have a moral obligation to receive our healing and health. To not receive it shows a lack of appreciation of all that Jesus went through on the cross so that we could live in divine health. It is really a slap in His face not to receive the benefits of healing and health.

> Psalm 105: 36, 37
> 36 He also destroyed all the firstborn in their land,
> The first of all their strength.
> 37 He also brought them out with silver and gold,
> AND THERE WAS NONE FEEBLE AMONG HIS TRIBES. (Emphasis added)

Here is further proof that God was Israel's healer under the Old Covenant. This is what happened to Israel after God delivered them out of Egypt, and there were millions of Jews that came out of Egypt. When God delivered them, Psalm 105:37 says, "He also brought them out with silver and gold, and there was none feeble among His tribes." The word *feeble* is referring to sickly people.

This is remarkable because we know that in Egypt, Israel was in bondage to hard taskmasters. They worked under very horrible conditions and were treated worse than slaves. We know that there were multitudes of sick people among them. Yet when God delivered them, there were none feeble among them. He supernaturally restored them to health.

> Psalm 107:20
> 20 He sent His word and healed them, And delivered them from their destructions.

God sent His Word and healed them and delivered them from their destruction. Under the Old Covenant, God healed through His Word. He is still healing people today through His Word.

John 1:1, 3, 14

1 In the beginning was the Word, and the Word was with God, and the Word was God.

3 All things were made through Him, and without Him nothing was made that was made.

14 And the Word became flesh and dwelt among us, and we beheld His glory, the glory as of the only begotten of the Father, full of grace and truth.

In verse 1, Word refers to the Lord Jesus Christ. It is translated in Greek as Logos, which means "the living Word." So, in the beginning was the Word (Jesus), and the Word (Jesus) was with God, and the Word (Jesus) was God. Verse 3 says, "All things were made through Him [the Word], and without Him [the Word] nothing was made that was made." Verse 14 says, "And the Word [Jesus] became flesh and dwelt among us, and we beheld His glory."

Psalm 107:20 says, "He sent His word and healed them." Jesus, the Word, became flesh and dwelt among us. In His great ministry on the earth, Jesus healed the sick. God healed the sick through His Word (Jesus). He sent His Word (Jesus) and healed them.

God is still healing through His Word today. And He's doing it through the written Word. For example, in Matthew 8:17 it says, "He Himself...bore our sicknesses." First Peter 2:24 says, "By whose stripes you were healed."

God's Best Is Not Divine Healing; God's Best Is Divine Health

When you receive that Word and act upon it, God will heal you by the Word. And God's Word will not only heal you but will also cause you to live a life of divine health. You see, God's best is not divine healing—God's best is divine health. Let me show you a revelation that I received concerning this from Proverbs 4:20 thru 22.

A Foundation for Healing

> Proverbs 4:20-22
>
> 20 My son, give attention to my words; Incline your ear to my sayings.
>
> 21 Do not let them depart from your eyes; Keep them in the midst of your heart;
>
> 22 For they are life to those who find them, AND HEALTH TO ALL THEIR FLESH. (Emphasis added)

As I was teaching this passage one day, I suddenly saw something I had never seen before. It was in here all the time, but I never saw it in this light before. That is why when you go to the Word of God, you should never take for granted that you know everything you need to know about a particular scripture. There is always more to glean from the Word. God's Word is pregnant, and it constantly gives birth to new facets of revelation knowledge. It is like a gold mine from which you can never exhaust all of its rich treasures.

I have been reading this verse for years, and I never saw this before. Verse 20 says, "My son, give attention to my words; Incline your ear to my sayings." Verse 21 says, "Do not let them [God's words and sayings] depart from your eyes; Keep them [God's words and sayings] in the midst of your heart; For they [God's words and sayings] are life to those who find them, And health to all their flesh."

Notice what it does not say in verse 22. It does not say the Word is healing to all their flesh (although it is healing, no doubt about that). This verse reveals something far greater than the fact that the Word is healing to all of our flesh—the Word is health to all our flesh. This verse is pointing us to God's best, which is beyond the realm of divine healing; it is the realm of divine health. When you are in the realm of divine health, you do not need healing because you are healthy.

How to Resist Sickness

> 3 John 2
>
> 2 Beloved, I pray that you may prosper in all things and be in health, just as your soul prospers.

God wants us to prosper in all things and be in health instead of constantly getting sick and having to get healed over and over again. He wants us to be in health.

That does not mean that you will never get attacked with sickness and disease. But when it comes, you can resist it in the Name of Jesus. Sickness and disease do not belong to you. You do what James 4:7 says, "Therefore submit to God. Resist the devil and he will flee from you." The word *flee* means to run as in terror.

You resist the devil by resisting everything he sends your way, which includes sickness and disease. So when Satan acts like the UPS man, knocks on your door with a package of sickness and disease, hands you the clipboard, and asks you to sign for the package, you simply refuse. Tell him, "I am not going to sign for it. It is not mine. Take it elsewhere because this package of sickness and disease does not belong to me."

On the other hand, if you say, "Well, I guess I am coming down with a cold," or, "My arthritis is acting up again," without realizing it, you have signed for the package on the dotted line. Satan will leave that package with you because you accepted it.

What you must do is refuse to sign the package by saying, "No Satan, I resist you. I refuse to accept this arthritis. I refuse to accept this cold or flu. I refuse to accept this backache, headache or whatever the sickness." By doing that you are resisting the devil, and he will flee from you. He'll get right back into his truck and drive off.

Let us back up to verse 20 and look at this passage more carefully. "My son, give attention to my words." That means to give the Word of God your undivided attention. Put the Word of God first place in your life.

Continuing with this verse, it says, "Incline your ear to my sayings." There is a good reason why we should do this. Romans 10:17 says, "So then faith comes by hearing, and hearing by the word of God." That is why we need to hear the Word of God—so that faith will come. Faith is inspired, charged, and uplifted when you hear the Word of God. Keep hearing the Word of God. Incline your ear to God's sayings.

Verse 21 says, "Do not let them [God's words and sayings] depart from your eyes." Keep reading the Word of God so that revelation knowledge will come to you. Keep them in the midst of your heart. The way you do this is by meditating on the Word. Meditating on

God's Word will cause the Word to take root in you so that you will have a solid foundation. Dig deep into the Word of God and get the foundation of God's Word in your heart.

God's Word Is Medicine and You Must Take It for It to Work

Verse 22 gives us the reason why we should do all of the things mentioned in verses 20 and 21, "For they [God's words and sayings] are life to those who find them." To find them, you have to look for them. You have to take the initiative to get into the Word and find out what it says. When you do that, they become life to you and health to your flesh.

The Word will produce health to your flesh. The Hebrew word for health is medicine. The Word is medicine to your flesh. It is medicine for your body. It is just like medicine in the natural. If the doctor prescribes medication for you, you must take it for it to do you any good. And you cannot hit and miss sporadically; you must take it regularly.

Now when it comes to healing, you must constantly feed along the lines of faith and healing. You will always need faith and healing throughout your whole Christian life. Once you have found the healing scriptures in the Word of God and have studied the Word on healing, go over those scriptures time and time again. Do not make the mistake that some people make when they think they already know everything about healing. They feel they do not have to go back and study those scriptures again. The Word is medicine.

Suppose you were to go to the doctor and he prescribed medication for you to take over a period of six months. If he prescribes the same medication for you six months later, are you going to tell the doctor, "I am not going to take this medication because I had it six months ago. I want something new"? No! You are going to listen to what the doctor tells you, and you will take that medication again. The same medicine that was good for you six months ago will be good for you six months from now.

Well, the same thing is true with the Word of God. The same healing scriptures that you need right now, you will need six months from now, a year from now, five years from now, ten years from now, etc. You do not need anything new.

Now I am not saying you should not study other Bible subjects. I am not saying that at all. You need to do that. In fact, the same principle we are applying to healing will work for any Bible subject. You need to keep hearing the Word over and over and over again. But I believe that faith and healing are two subjects that you should constantly build yourself upon. When you know the Word in those areas, it will do you much good in your life and also bless and help others.

Healing Has Not Passed Away

Some people say that in the ministry of Jesus, He performed healings and miracles to prove that He was the Son of God. They use that to teach there is no need for healing and miracles today—that they both have passed away. But that simply is not true, and I want to prove that to you from the Word.

First of all, Jesus healed because it has always been God's will for His people to be well, healed, whole, and free from sickness and disease. Let me show you that Jesus did not heal to prove that He was the Son of God. Let us look at Mark 6:1-6.

> Mark 6:1-6
> 1 Then He went out from there and came to His own country, and His disciples followed Him.
> 2 And when the Sabbath had come, He began to teach in the synagogue. And many hearing Him were astonished, saying, "Where did this Man get these things? And what wisdom is this which is given to Him, that such mighty works are performed by His hands!
> 3 "Is this not the carpenter, the Son of Mary, and brother of James, Joses, Judas, and Simon? And are not His sisters here with us?" So they were offended at Him.

> 4 But Jesus said to them, "A prophet is not without honor except in his own country, among his own relatives, and in his own house."
> 5 Now He could do no mighty work there, except that He laid His hands on a few sick people and healed them.
> 6 And He marveled because of their unbelief. Then He went about the villages in a circuit, teaching.

Jesus was ministering in His hometown. Verse 5 says that He could do no mighty work there. It did not say that He would do no mighty work there. It said that He could do no mighty work there. There is a difference between would not and could not. If it had said He would not, that would indicate He refused to heal anybody there. But it does not say He would not. It says that He could not. That means He could not heal anybody there.

The Bible says in verse 5, "Now He could do no mighty work there, except that He laid His hands on a few sick people and healed them." Verse 6 gives us some insight as to why He could not heal them. It says, "And He marveled because of their unbelief." Unbelief stopped Jesus from doing any mighty work there, even though He had the ability to heal the sick and work miracles. If unbelief hindered the power of God then, it will hinder the power of God now. People's unbelief today is the reason why many do not receive healing from God.

Jesus Did Not Heal the Sick as the Son of God

Now here is the point I want to make. If Jesus was healing to prove that He was the Son of God, why did He not do any mighty work there? It says that He did no mighty works. We know that Jesus did mighty works in other places, but not there—not in His own hometown. That also shows us that Jesus did not heal and perform miracles because He was the Son of God.

Philippians 2:7 (AMP)
7 But stripped Himself [of all privileges and rightful dignity], so as to assume the guise of a servant (slave), in that He became like men and was born a human being.

Philippians, Chapter 2, tells us that He stripped Himself of His deity when He became flesh and dwelt among us. He laid aside His deity, and He ministered as a man anointed by the Holy Spirit. He did not minister as the Son of God. He was the Son of God, yet He was 100% God and 100% man. He laid aside His deity as the Son of God.

He ministered with the same equipment that believers have today which is the Word and the Spirit. You see, what many are doing is aborting the healing ministry today because they think they cannot do what Jesus did.

John 14:12
12 "Most assuredly, I say to you, he who believes in Me, the works that I do he will do also; and greater works than these he will do, because I go to My Father."

Jesus said, "Greater works than these he [you] will do, because I go to My Father." The greater works are greater works in quantity, not greater works in quality. We will never do better works in quality than He did, but we will do better works in quantity. When Jesus ministered to the sick, He could only be at one place at a time. The people that received healing from Jesus had to be where He was to receive it, or they had to be where those He commissioned to minister to the sick were. At that time, He was the only one in whom the Spirit of God dwelt.

After Jesus' death, burial, and resurrection, He delegated authority to the Church—those who would receive Him as the Lord of their lives. We as Christians have the delegated authority to do the works that Jesus did. When we receive the gift of the Holy Spirit, He empowers us by His Spirit to do those works.

Every believer has been commissioned according to Mark 16:17 and 18 to lay hands on the sick. When Jesus ministered on the earth, everybody had to be where He was for Him to minister to them. But Christ has duplicated Himself in every believer. Today, there are believers all across the face of this earth who are ministering to the sick. This explains how we can do greater works than Jesus in quantity.

The Church, however, has placed the ministry of Jesus on a pedestal where it does not belong. Now do not misunderstand me. Jesus Christ as the Son of God belongs on a pedestal high above us all, but what I am referring to is the ministry of Jesus. Jesus did not minister as the Son of God—He ministered as a man anointed by the Spirit. The ministry of Jesus does not belong in a class all by itself. We can attain the same ministry of Jesus, which includes healing.

"Do you mean to tell me that we can do the works that Jesus did?" I did not say that, the Bible says that in John 14:12. "The works that I do he will do also." Who will do the works? "He [you] who believes in Me [Jesus], the works that I [Jesus] do he [you] will do also."

"Well, I do not believe that we can do the works that He did." Well, you have just disqualified yourself because it only happens to those who believe. It says, "He who believes in Me, the works that I do he will do also; and greater works than those he will do, because I go to My Father." Mark 16:17 and 18 says, "And these signs will follow those who believe...they will lay hands on the sick, and they will recover."

You mean that believers can lay hands on the sick and they can get well?" That is what Jesus said, and I believe Jesus tells the truth. "[God] is not a man, that He should lie." (Numbers 23:19).

Now man can lie to you, and he can tell you that healing went out with the last apostle. But I would rather believe Jesus. I would rather believe what the Word says. Man can lie, seminaries can lie, denominations can lie but Jesus cannot lie. Jesus Christ is still in the healing business.

"Well, (some may say) I still do not believe that we can lay hands on the sick today and see them get well." Again, you have just disqualified yourself because it only happens to those who believe. The same way we receive salvation is the same way we receive healing. You do not wait to experience salvation before you believe it. You have to believe in salvation before you can experience salvation.

The same principle applies to healing. You have to believe that you are healed before you can experience healing. If you wait to experience healing before you believe it, you will never get healed. It is as simple as that. These things are so simple, yet many times people stumble over them.

I will give further proof that Jesus did not heal because He was the Son of God. When He was a child, Jesus sat in the temple and asked questions of the theologians. But no miracles or healings took place until He was baptized by John the Baptist in the Jordan River at the age of thirty. From the time He was born to the time He was baptized, there were no miracles, no healings, and no mighty works.

Now let me ask you a question. Was Jesus the Son of God when He was five, ten, and fifteen years old? Yes, of course, He was! Jesus was just as much the Son of God when He was five as when He was thirty. Yet He did not do any mighty works until He was baptized, and the Spirit of God came upon Him. He could not minister until He was anointed. My point is this, if He ministered as the Son of God, He would have done miracles, healings, and mighty works before He was anointed with the Holy Spirit.

In His own hometown, Jesus could do no mighty works there. As we said earlier, it was not that He would do no mighty works—He could do no mighty works. If Jesus healed the sick in His ministry to prove that He was the Son of God, then certainly He would have done it there.

Hebrews 4:15 says, "For we do not have a High Priest who cannot sympathize with our weaknesses, but was in all points tempted as we are, yet without sin." That is basically saying that Jesus can relate to us. He can relate to our weaknesses because He walked this earth. He faced the same temptations that you and I face today.

Although He was God, He was also human. If you really want to make a good showing, you will want to do it in your hometown. So I am sure that Jesus wanted to do good in His hometown. In other words, if He performed miracles and healings to prove that He was the Son of God, then certainly He would have wanted to do it where He grew up. But he could not do it because of the people's unbelief. They were too familiar with Him and looked upon Him as the little boy who grew up there. They did not recognize His ministry and the anointing on His life, so He could not do any mighty works there.

He was the Son of God in His hometown, but He did not minister out of His deity. He ministered as a man anointed by the Spirit. Jesus did not heal because He was the Son of God. He healed because it was God's will for people to be well, and it pleased the Father for people to be well. Jesus did only what He saw the Father do, and He always did those things that pleased the Father. He had the same compassion for the sick as did His Father God. In this compassion, He ministered to the sick so that they could be healed.

The Redemptive Names of God

The Scofield Bible defines the redemptive names of God. The name Jehovah is distinctly the redemptive name of deity and means the self-existent one who reveals Himself.

In His redemptive relation to man, Jehovah has seven compound names which reveal God as meeting every need of man. One of His redemptive names is Jehovah Rapha, which means I am the Lord that heals you.

Here are the other redemptive names and what they reveal: Jehovah-Shammah, the Lord is present; Jehovah-Shalom, the Lord our peace; Jehovah-Rohi, the Lord is my Shepherd; Jehovah-Jireh, the Lord who foresees and the Lord will provide; Jehovah Nissi, the Lord our Banner; and Jehovah-Tsidkenu, the Lord our Righteousness.

Since these are redemptive names, the blessing that each name reveals must be provided in the redemption of Christ. These names find their fulfillment in Jesus Christ our Redeemer. All of the benefits that God's redemptive names reveal are made available to us through the death, burial, and resurrection of our Lord Jesus Christ. The name Jehovah Rapha means "Jesus is our Healer."

An Ordinance of Healing

"This name is given to us to reveal our redemptive privilege of being healed. The very first covenant God gave after delivering His people from the Red Sea (which was typical of our redemption in Christ) was the covenant of healing. It was at this time that God revealed Himself as our Physician. This is the first redemptive and covenant name: Jehovah Rapha, I am the Lord that healeth you. This is not only a promise, it is a statute and an ordinance. We have a corresponding ordinance of healing in the new covenant, and it is just as sacred and binding as the ordinances of the Lord's supper and water baptism."[1]

We find that ordinance in the book of James.

> James 5:14
> 14 Is anyone among you sick? Let him call for the elders of the church, and let them pray over him, anointing him with oil in the name of the Lord.

James asks, "Is anyone among you sick?" This implies that there should not be any sick among us. In case there is any, this is an open invitation for anyone in the Church (this letter is written to the Church) to come and receive their healing.

Hebrews 8:6 says that we live in a better covenant established upon better promises. If God had a covenant of healing in the Old Covenant, then certainly He must have it in this New Covenant. We have a better covenant established upon better promises. For this New Covenant to be better, it must at least have what the old had or else it would not be better, would it?

---

[1] F.F. Bosworth, *Christ the Healer*, (Grand Rapids: Baker Book House Company, 1993) p. 23.

4.
Jesus Was the Will of God in Action

Let us talk about Jesus Christ, the will of God in action. If you want to know what the will of God is, look at Jesus. If you want to know God's purpose, look at Jesus. If you want to know God's character, look at Jesus. When He walked the earth, Jesus Christ was the will of God in action. In fact, Jesus never took credit for any miracles or healings that He did.

> John 14:8,9
> 8 Philip said to Him, "Lord, show us the Father, and it is sufficient for us."
> 9 Jesus said to him, "Have I been with you so long, and yet you have not known Me, Philip? He who has seen Me has seen the Father; so how can you say, 'Show us the Father'?"

Jesus says in verse 9, "He who has seen Me has seen the Father." So in essence, what Jesus is saying is this, if you want to know what the Father looks like, look at Me. In John 14:10, Jesus goes on to say, "The Father who dwells in Me does the works." The Father was carrying out His will through His Son Jesus Christ. When you look at Jesus, you are looking at the Father because Jesus was the will of God in action.

> John 8:29
> 29 "And He who sent Me is with Me. The Father has not left Me alone, for I always do those things that please Him."

Jesus says here, "I always do those things that please Him." And what are some of the things that Jesus did that pleased Him? He went about doing good and healing all who were oppressed by the devil, according to Acts 10:38. Since Jesus always did those things that pleased the Father, it must have pleased the Father greatly to see sick people receive their healing. When Jesus went about healing the multitudes, He gave His heavenly Father joy.

Notice something significant about the healing ministry of Jesus. Jesus never put sickness or disease on anyone. That tells us that it must not be God putting sickness on people.

Some say that God puts sickness on people. Well, first of all, He cannot do that because He does not have any sickness to give you. Furthermore, if it pleased God to put sickness on people, then Jesus would have put sickness on people since He was the will of God in action.

In addition, it must not please God to see people remain sick. Every person who came to Jesus received their healing—He never turned anyone away. Jesus never refused to heal anybody. That lets us know that it must please the Father to heal everyone who comes to Him for healing. Jesus always did those things that pleased the Father.

> John 8:38
> 38 "I speak what I have seen with My Father, and you
> do what you have seen with your father."

Jesus says, "I speak what I have seen with My Father." Now, remember, Jesus was in the beginning with God. He has been with God from eternity. He observed the Father's dealings with the children of Israel under the Old Covenant. He says here, "I speak what I have seen with My Father." When Jesus spoke healing to people, He did so because that is what He had seen with His Father. He saw healing with His Father; therefore, He spoke healing and ministered healing. Jesus never refused to heal anyone because He never saw the Father refuse to heal anyone.

Jesus Was the Will of God in Action

> John 5:19, 20
> 19 Then Jesus answered and said to them, "Most assuredly, I say to you, the Son can do nothing of Himself, but what He sees the Father do; for whatever He does, the Son also does in like manner.
> 20 "For the Father loves the Son, and shows Him all things that He Himself does, and He will show Him greater works than these, that you may marvel."

When Jesus went about healing the sick—healing all who were oppressed by the devil—He did that because He saw the Father doing it. Whatever He saw the Father do, the Son did in like manner.

Remember that God reveals Himself as the Healer. "For I am the LORD who heals you" (Exodus 15:26). Healer is one of God's redemptive names; and, since Jesus sees the Father healing, He heals in like manner. Jesus healed the sick because the Father taught Him how to heal the sick. God the Father shows Jesus all of the things He does, which includes healing the sick.

I believe the reason why we never see Jesus turning anyone away that came to Him for healing was because the Father never showed Him that He should turn anyone away. Every request that came to Jesus for healing was granted based on the faith of the individual.

Healing Is for All

> Matthew 4:23, 24
> 23 And Jesus went about all Galilee, teaching in their synagogues, preaching the gospel of the kingdom, and HEALING ALL KINDS OF SICKNESS AND ALL KINDS OF DISEASE AMONG THE PEOPLE. (Emphasis added)
> 24 Then His fame went throughout all Syria; and they brought to Him all sick people who were afflicted with various diseases and torments, and those who were demon-possessed, epileptics, and

paralytics; and HE HEALED THEM. (Emphasis added)

We notice from verse 23 that Jesus' ministry consisted of three primary things: teaching (Jesus always put teaching first), preaching, and healing. It says that He healed all kinds of sickness and all kinds of disease. It says here that He healed all sick people who were afflicted with various diseases and torments. He healed them all. How many did He heal? He healed ALL the sick people who were afflicted.

This is consistent with what we read in Acts 10:38. God anointed Jesus of Nazareth with the Holy Spirit and with power, after which Jesus went about doing good and healing all who were oppressed by the devil. All the people that He healed were satanically oppressed which tells us that sickness is indeed from the devil. And notice that out of this great multitude of people, Jesus did not leave one person sick—He healed them all.

> Matthew 8:16, 17
> 16 When evening had come, they brought to Him many who were demon-possessed. And He cast out the spirits with a word, and healed all who were sick, 17 that it might be fulfilled which was spoken by Isaiah the prophet, saying: "He Himself took our infirmities and bore our sicknesses."

Verse 16 tells us that Jesus healed all who were sick. Jesus healed everybody who was sick in the crowd without exception. We are seeing a scriptural pattern of Jesus healing everyone who came to Him in need of healing.

> Matthew 9:35
> 35 Then Jesus went about all the cities and villages, teaching in their synagogues, preaching the gospel of the kingdom, and healing every sickness and every disease among the people.

We see again that Jesus healed every sickness and every disease among the people. There was not one that He left who was still sick.

> Matthew 10:1
> 1 And when He had called His twelve disciples to Him, He gave them power over unclean spirits, to cast them out, and to heal all kinds of sickness and all kinds of disease.

We see that Jesus gave the disciples authority to heal all kinds of sickness and disease. Notice, He never told them to pray *if it be Thy will*. He never told them it may not be God's will to heal everyone that they prayed for. When Jesus gave them the power to heal all kinds of sickness and diseases, He gave them power over the work of the devil. Notice the words "power…to heal". Power…to heal all kinds of sickness and diseases tells us that it is God will for His power to eradicate and eliminate sickness and diseases. He gave His disciples unconditional power to heal all with absolutely no exceptions!

> Matthew 12:15
> 15 But when Jesus knew it, He withdrew from there. And great multitudes followed Him, and He healed them all.

Here, great multitudes followed Him and He healed them all. Everyone in this great multitude received their healing.

> Matthew 14:14
> 14 And when Jesus went out He saw a great multitude; and He was moved with compassion for them, and healed their sick.

Jesus saw the multitude and was moved with compassion for them and healed their sick. In other words, He healed all the sick in this great multitude.

> Matthew 14:34-36
> 34 When they had crossed over, they came to the land of Gennesaret.
> 35 And when the men of that place recognized Him, they sent out into all that surrounding region, brought to Him all who were sick,
> 36 and begged Him that they might only touch the hem of His garment. AND AS MANY AS TOUCHED IT WERE MADE PERFECTLY WELL. (Emphasis added)

The people in Gennesaret went out and gathered all of those who were sick. They had faith to believe that if they could only touch the hem of His garment, they would receive their healing. The verse says that as many as touched it was made perfectly well. Everyone who touched His garment received their healing.

Gifts of Healings

> Luke 4:40
> 40 When the sun was setting, all those who had any that were sick with various diseases brought them to Him; and He laid His hands on every one of them and healed them.

Again, all the sick were brought to Jesus, and He laid His hands on every one of them and healed them.

> Luke 6:19 says, "And the whole multitude sought to touch Him [Jesus], for power went out from Him and healed them all." Jesus healed all who were sick among the multitude.

We have looked at several passages in which Jesus healed all who came to Him for healing. Now let us look at another aspect of Jesus' ministry. People think that Jesus just went around and indiscriminately healed everyone in sight, but this was not the case. We saw an example of that in Jesus hometown, where He was unable to do any mighty works. He had a special anointing to minister to the sick. Everyone who came in faith received their healing. However, when gifts of healings were in operation in Jesus' ministry, only the people that the Holy Spirit singled out were healed.

> John 5:1-9
> 1 After this there was a feast of the Jews, and Jesus went up to Jerusalem.
> 2 Now there is in Jerusalem by the Sheep Gate a pool, which is called in Hebrew, Bethesda, having five porches.
> 3 In these lay a great multitude of sick people, blind, lame, paralyzed, waiting for the moving of the water.
> 4 For an angel went down at a certain time into the pool and stirred up the water; then whoever stepped in first, after the stirring of the water, was made well of whatever disease he had.
> 5 Now a certain man was there who had an infirmity thirty-eight years.
> 6 When Jesus saw him lying there, and knew that he already had been in that condition a long time, He said to him, "Do you want to be made well?"
> 7 The sick man answered Him, "Sir, I have no man to put me into the pool when the water is stirred up; but while I am coming, another steps down before me."
> 8 Jesus said to him, "Rise, take up your bed and walk."
> 9 And immediately the man was made well, took up his bed, and walked. And that day was the Sabbath.

Remember, Jesus did not minister as the Son of God even though He was the Son of God when He walked the earth. He was 100% God and 100% man. But according to Philippians, Chapter 2, He laid aside His deity. In other words, He stripped Himself of His divine power. Therefore, He ministered as a man anointed by the Spirit, not as the Son of God.

In John, Chapter 5, we see an example of gifts of healings in operation. There was a pool called Bethesda that had five porches. A great multitude of sick people—blind, lame, and paralyzed—gathered around the pool and waited for the moving or touching of the water. An angel would go down every so often into the pool and stir up the water. Whoever got in the water first, after the angel had stirred it up, was made well of whatever disease he had.

There was a man there who had an infirmity for thirty-eight years. Jesus asked him in verse 6, "Do you want to be made well?" In verse 7, the sick man replied, "Sir, I have no man to put me into the pool when the water is stirred up; but while I am coming, another steps down before me." Jesus said to him, "Rise, take up your bed and walk." Verse 9 states, "And immediately the man was made well, took up his bed, and walked."

Jesus went to a pool that had five porches full of sick people. In fact, there was "a great multitude of people." Now, this is the point I want you to see: Jesus only ministered to one sick person among the whole multitude because gifts of healings were in operation.

When gifts of healings are in operation, only the person or people who the Holy Spirit singles out will be healed. The Holy Spirit only directed Jesus to one person. He left all of the rest of that multitude at the pool sick.

Now there is no question in my mind that if those people around the pool had recognized Jesus and released their faith, they would have received their healing also. But that did not happen because they did not realize it was Jesus. Even the man who was healed did not know (at first) that it was Jesus who healed him. Therefore, it was not possible for them to exercise their faith for healing, because faith comes by hearing the Word (Romans 10:17). Jesus is the Word, so they could not have released their faith in the Word, because they did not know the Word was in their midst. And that is how we know it was the gifts of healings that got the man healed. He did not get healed because of his faith in Jesus because the man did not even know it was Jesus.

In John 5:12, the Jews asked this man, "Who is the Man who said to you, 'Take up your bed and walk'?" Verse 13 says, "But the one who was healed did not know who it was, for Jesus had withdrawn, a multitude being in that place." So none of the sick people there knew that it was Jesus. But gifts of the Spirit were in operation, and the Holy Spirit directed Jesus to only one man. He healed the man and left the rest of them sick. Therefore, Jesus did not go around healing every sick person that He saw.

Faith Required

Some people ask, "Why aren't people healed automatically like they were in the ministry of Jesus?" Some people assume that healing always takes place automatically without requiring the individual to have any responsibility. But if you examine the four gospels, you will find that in most cases it requires faith of the individual for them to receive their healing. Let us look at a couple of examples.

> Luke 17:11-16
> 11 Now it happened as He went to Jerusalem that He passed through the midst of Samaria and Galilee.
> 12 Then as He entered a certain village, there met Him ten men who were lepers, who stood afar off.
> 13 And they lifted up their voices and said, "Jesus, Master, have mercy on us!"
> 14 So when He saw them, He said to them, "Go, show yourselves to the priests." And so it was that as they went, they were cleansed.
> 15 And one of them, when he saw that he was healed, returned, and with a loud voice glorified God,
> 16 and fell down on his face at His feet, giving Him thanks. And he was a Samaritan.

Ten lepers came to Jesus and said to Him, "Jesus, Master, have mercy on us!" Verse 14 says, "So when He saw them, He said to them, 'Go, show yourselves to the priests.'"

They were not healed automatically. They had no physical change in their bodies, but Jesus gave them something to act on. When Jesus said, "Go, show yourselves to the priests," they were healed as far as Jesus was concerned. Their healing was a fact in the spirit realm.

To receive their healing, however, they had to be obedient and act on the word that Jesus said to them. He told them to show themselves to the priests, and they went on their way. In other words, they acted on the Word. It says in verse 14, "And so it was that as they went, they were cleansed."

When Jesus told them to show themselves to the priests, they were still lepers. When they started on their way to the priests, they were still lepers. But as they went or as they were going to the priests, these lepers received the manifestation of their healing. As they went, they were cleansed!

Had they not left, they would not have been cleansed. Had they just sat there and did nothing, they would not have been healed. They could have argued with Jesus and said, "We are not going to show ourselves to the priests. We will get stoned and persecuted if we go to the priests! Being lepers, we are not to go to the priests until we are healed. So unless you heal us, we are not going!" If they had that kind of attitude, they would not have been healed.

By faith, these lepers began to go as Jesus instructed. He simply said, "Go, show yourselves to the priests." There was no physical evidence of healing in their bodies, but they acted in faith and began to go. As they went, they received their healing.

Let us look at another example whereby healing did not occur automatically.

> John 4:46-52
> 46 So Jesus came again to Cana of Galilee where He had made the water wine. And there was a certain nobleman whose son was sick at Capernaum.
> 47 When he heard that Jesus had come out of Judea into Galilee, he went to Him and implored Him to

come down and heal his son, for he was at the point of death.

48 Then Jesus said to him, "Unless you people see signs and wonders, you will by no means believe."

49 The nobleman said to Him, "Sir, come down before my child dies!"

50 Jesus said to him, "Go your way; your son lives." So the man believed the word that Jesus spoke to him, and he went his way.

51 And as he was now going down, his servants met him and told him, saying, "Your son lives!"

52 Then he inquired of them the hour when he got better. And they said to him, "Yesterday at the seventh hour the fever left him."

There was a nobleman whose son was sick at Capernaum. When he heard that Jesus was at Galilee, he went to Jesus and asked Him to come and heal his son who was at the point of death. Verse 49 states, "The nobleman said to Him, 'Sir, come down before my child dies!'" Jesus spoke the word of faith to him and said, "Go your way; your son lives." That was the word of Jesus to the man.

Remember that the man was not where his son was at the time. His son was at home, and the man went away from his home to Galilee to see Jesus. When Jesus said, "Your son lives," the man could not look at his son to see whether or not he was healed since his son was not there.

But here is a remarkable and commendable thing; the man believed the Word. Verse 50 says, "So the man believed the word that Jesus spoke to him, and he went his way." He did not ask Jesus for a sign. He obeyed Jesus in simple faith and went his way just as Jesus told him to do.

Verse 51 says, "And as he was now going down." That sounds like what the lepers did. The Bible says concerning the lepers, "And so it was that as they went, they were cleansed" (Luke 17:14). Likewise, as the nobleman was going down—as he acted on the word that Jesus spoke to him—his servants met him and told him saying, "Your son lives."

The nobleman asked his servants when did his son get better. The King James version says in verse 52, "Then inquired he of them the hour when he began to amend." Since the healing process began in his son's body, he did not get healed instantly. He went from a point of being sick to a point of being well. Jesus said in Mark 16:18, "They will lay hands on the sick, and they will recover." The word *recovery* implies a process of going from a point of being sick to a point of being well.

Notice that the nobleman asked his servants when his son got better or when he began to amend. He was not instantly healed, but he began to amend. In John 4:52, his servants answered, "Yesterday at the seventh hour the fever left him."

Apparently, there were other things wrong with him beside the fever. The healing process began as the fever left him. So he got better and better until he received the full manifestation of his healing.

Verse 52 says, "And they said to him, 'Yesterday at the seventh hour the fever left him.'" Verse 53 says, "So the father knew that it was at the same hour in which Jesus said to him, 'Your son lives.' And he himself believed, and his whole household." So we see that all healing is not automatic. The lepers were healed as they went, and the nobleman's son began to heal as his father believed and acted on Jesus' word.

5.
The Purpose of Preaching and Teaching

The number one purpose for preaching and teaching is to produce beliefs. Now when I talk about producing beliefs, I am talking about producing faith. Teaching and preaching the Word will build faith in people.

> Mark 16:15, 16
> 15 And He said to them,"Go into all the world and preach the gospel to every creature.
> 16 "He who believes and is baptized will be saved; but he who does not believe will be condemned."

We are to preach the gospel so that people will believe.

> Romans 10:6, 7
> 6 But the righteousness of faith speaks in this way, "Do not say in your heart, 'Who will ascend into heaven?'" (that is, to bring Christ down from above)
> 7 or, "'Who will descend into the abyss?'" (that is, to bring Christ up from the dead).

A lot of people say, "Oh, I wish Jesus was here." The Bible says, do not say in your heart, "Who will ascend into heaven?" (to bring Christ down from above). Faith does not ask for Jesus to come down out of heaven. Here is what the Word of faith says:

Romans 10:8-11, 13-15

8 But what does it say? "The word is near you, in your mouth and in your heart" (that is, the word of faith which we preach):

9 that if you confess with your mouth the Lord Jesus and believe in your heart that God has raised Him from the dead, you will be saved.

10 For with the heart one believes unto righteousness, and with the mouth confession is made unto salvation.

11 For the Scriptures says, "Whoever believes on Him will not be put to shame."

13 For "whoever calls on the name of the LORD shall be saved."

14 How then shall they call on Him in whom they have not believed? And how shall they believe in Him of whom they have not heard? And how shall they hear without a preacher?

15 And how shall they preach unless they are sent? As it is written:

"How beautiful are the feet of those who preach the gospel of

peace, Who bring glad tidings of good things!"

I know what it means when it says, "How beautiful are the feet of those who preach the gospel of peace, who bring glad tidings of good things!" Now let me show you why this is true. There is a reason why the feet of those who preach the gospel are so beautiful. We are going to read verses 13 and 14 in reverse. The number one purpose of preaching and teaching is to produce beliefs.

Reading Romans 10:14 in reverse it says, "And how shall they hear without a preacher? And how shall they believe in Him of whom they have not heard? How then shall they call on Him in whom they have not believed?

You see it all boils down to preaching and teaching. Do you follow me? Verse 13 says, "For whoever calls on the name of the LORD shall be saved." Before you call, you have to believe. A prerequisite for calling is believing. But before you believe, you must hear. And without a preacher, how shall they hear? That is why we have to preach the Word. That is why preaching is so important. Romans 10:17 says, "So then faith comes by hearing, and hearing by the word of God."

Without a preacher, how shall they hear? Without hearing how shall they believe? Now that is not just for salvation—that is for anything. Without hearing, how is a person going to believe? How is a person going to exercise their faith if they do not hear what the Word has to say? Without believing, how shall they call? And without calling, how shall they be saved? The definition of salvation includes healing so we could say, "Without calling, how shall they be healed."

You know what? It is very easy to get people to believe. A lot of times, people are mixed up; they are confused because of a lack of teaching. But you can get most people to believe as long as they are open to receive what the Word is saying.

> Acts 8:26-31
>
> 26 Now an angel of the Lord spoke to Philip, saying, "Arise and go toward the south along the road which goes down from Jerusalem to Gaza." This is desert.
>
> 27 So he arose and went. And behold, a man of Ethiopia, a eunuch of great authority under Candace the queen of the Ethiopians, who had charge of all her treasury, and had come to Jerusalem to worship,
>
> 28 was returning. And sitting in his chariot, he was reading Isaiah the prophet.
>
> 29 Then the Spirit said to Philip, "Go near and overtake this chariot."
>
> 30 So Philip ran to him, and heard him reading the prophet Isaiah, and said, "Do you understand what you are reading?"
>
> 31 And he said, "HOW CAN I, UNLESS SOMEONE GUIDES ME?" And he asked Philip to come up and sit with him. (Emphasis added)

The Spirit of the Lord directed Philip to go to the chariot. Philip got up on the chariot and started preaching to the eunuch. The eunuch was reading out of Isaiah. Philip asked him, "Do you understand what you are reading?" And the eunuch said, "How can I, unless someone guides me?"

The eunuch invited Philip to sit with him. Philip then began to explain the scripture to him. Verses 35 thru 37 says:

"Then Philip opened his mouth, and beginning at this Scripture, preached Jesus to him. Now as they went down the road, they came to some water. And the eunuch said, 'See, here is water. What hinders me from being baptized?' Then Philip said, 'If you believe with all your heart, you may.' And he answered and said, 'I believe that Jesus Christ is the Son of God.'"

The purpose of Philip's preaching was to produce a belief. Philip said, "If you believe with all your heart, you may [be baptized]." And the eunuch said, "I believe."

How does a person get saved? The Bible says according to Romans 10:9, 10 that if you confess with your mouth the Lord Jesus and believe in your heart that God has raised Him from the dead, you will be saved. Someone may have never heard the Word before, but when they believe that it is God's will to save them, and they act on it—by believing in their heart and confessing with their mouth—they are instantly saved!

It is easy to believe. The eunuch believed. He said, "I believe that Jesus Christ is the Son of God." When Philip preached Jesus to him, faith came because faith comes by hearing and hearing by the Word of God. Faith was present for that man to receive his salvation. He said, "I believe that Jesus Christ is the Son of God."

> Matthew 9:27, 28
> 27 When Jesus departed from there, two blind men followed Him, crying out and saying, "Son of David, have mercy on us!"
> 28 And when He had come into the house, the blind men came to Him. And Jesus said to them, "Do you

The Purpose of Preaching and Teaching

believe that I am able to do this?" They said to Him, "Yes, Lord."

Two blind men came to Jesus for healing. He said to them in verse 28, "'Do you believe that I am able to do this?' They said to Him, 'Yes, Lord.'" If they had said, "No, I do not believe," they would not have been healed. In most cases in Jesus' ministry, it took people's faith to receive their healing. They had to have faith to be healed.

Sometimes people think that Jesus just went around and indiscriminately healed anyone and everyone. That is not true. In most cases, people had to receive their healing by their own faith. Faith releases the healing power of God. Faith moves the hand of God. And faith speaks. Faith is released by words through your mouth.

> Matthew 9:29
> 29 Then He touched their eyes, saying, "According to your faith let it be to you."

The blind men released their faith by saying, "Yes, Lord." They simply acted on what they believed. Then Jesus healed them according to their faith.

Strengthening Beliefs

The second purpose of preaching and teaching is to strengthen beliefs. Now, this is very important. When you hear the Word on any particular subject, you can sense that you are receiving strength from the Word of God in that area. What is happening is that your beliefs are strengthened because of preaching and teaching.

> Acts 14:19-22
> 19 Then Jews from Antioch and Iconium came there; and having persuaded the multitudes, they stoned Paul and dragged him out of the city, supposing him to be dead.

> 20 However, when the disciples gathered around him, he rose up and went into the city. And the next day he departed with Barnabas to Derbe.
> 21 And when they had preached the gospel to that city and made many disciples, they returned to Lystra, Iconium, and Antioch,
> 22 STRENGTHENING THE SOULS of the disciples, exhorting them to continue in the faith, and saying, "We must through many tribulations enter the kingdom of God." (Emphasis added)

Paul went back to places where He had been before. He went back to do what? He went back to strengthen the souls of the disciples—to strengthen what they believed. They went there the first time to plant the seed of the Word. But they returned because they knew the value of watering the seed. Preaching and teaching will strengthen a person's beliefs.

> Acts 15:36, 40, 41
> 36 Then after some days Paul said to Barnabas, "Let us now go back and visit our brethren in every city where we have preached the word of the Lord, and see how they are doing."
> 40 but Paul chose Silas and departed, being commended by the brethren to the grace of God.
> 41 And he went through Syria and Cilicia, strengthening the churches.

These people were already born again, but they needed to be strengthened. Their beliefs needed to be strengthened. Now that brings us to another question, "What is the purpose of beliefs?"

The Purpose of Beliefs Is to Govern What We Think, Say, and Do

> Joshua 1:8
> 8 "This Book of the Law shall not depart from your mouth, but you shall meditate in it day and night, that you may observe to do according to all that is written in it. For then you will make your way prosperous, and then you will have good success."

What you believe will do you no good unless you allow it to govern what you think, say, and do. Allow the Word to dominate your thought life by meditating on the Word day and night. Keeping the Word in your mouth is letting the Word govern what you say.

This verse tells you why you should meditate in the Word—so that you may observe to do. Observe to do what? Observe to do all that is written. That is allowing the Word to govern what you do. By keeping the Word in your mouth, meditating in it day and night, and acting on it, you will make your way prosperous; and you will have good success.

6.
Roadblocks to Healing

Now we are going to discuss roadblocks to healing. There are certain roadblocks—stumbling blocks—that get in people's way when it comes to the subject of healing. And these roadblocks will hinder you and keep you from hearing what God has to say concerning your healing.

Roadblock #1—Job

Many people have this question concerning their healing. "What about Job? Wasn't Job a sick man all of his life?" Many theologians agree that the entire book of Job took place during a period of nine months to a year. Therefore, what you read in the book of Job is not about an entire lifetime of the man. Whatever Job went through, it did not last all of his life. All of the afflictions that Job went through lasted no more than one year.

Be careful when you say you are just another Job because we are going to show you from the Word of God that Job was a blessed man. In fact, he was an extremely blessed man. After he went through his brief affliction, he ended up with more than he had before his trials.

> Job 1:6-7
> 6 Now there was a day when the sons of God came to present themselves before the LORD, and Satan also came among them.
> 7 And the LORD said to Satan, "From where do you come?" So Satan answered the LORD and said, "From going to and fro on the earth, and from walking back and forth on it."

That is still what Satan does today according to 1 Peter 5:8. "The devil walks about like a roaring lion, seeking whom he may devour." Notice, it says Satan is seeking those whom he may devour. The word *may* denotes permission. In other words, Satan goes around seeking those who give him the opportunity to devour them. Satan cannot devour you unless you allow him to or give him permission to do so.

> Job 1:8-10
> 8 Then the LORD said to Satan, "Have you considered My servant Job, that there is none like him on the earth, a blameless and upright man, one who fears God and shuns evil?"
> 9 So Satan answered the LORD and said, "Does Job fear God for nothing?
> 10 "Have You not made a hedge around him, around his household, and around all that he has on every side? You have blessed the work of his hands, and his possessions have increased in the land.

It is interesting to note that Satan knew that God had a hedge around Job, his household, and his possessions. Do you know that God has a hedge around every Christian? Now let us find out how the hedge can be pulled down. This passage also gives us some insight into the nature of Satan.

> Job 1:11-12
> 11 "But now, stretch out Your hand and touch all that he has, and he will surely curse You to Your face!"
> 12 And the LORD said to Satan, "Behold, all that he has is in your power; only do not lay a hand on his person." So Satan went out from the presence of the LORD.

Starting in verse 11, Satan says, " 'But now, stretch out Your hand and touch all that he has [or destroy all that he has], and he [Job] will surely curse You [God] to Your face!' And the LORD said to Satan, 'Behold, all that he has is in your power; only do not lay a hand on his person.' So Satan went out from the presence of the LORD. ' "

Satan is asking God to touch or destroy what Job had. But that is not the nature of God. God does not take away as some interpret from the book of Job. God does not take away; He is a giver. It is Satan who takes away according to John 10:10.

Now some people interpret verse 12 as saying that the Lord gave Satan permission to attack Job, but this was not the case. The Lord simply said to him "all that he has is in your power."

Adam was the original god of this world. He was given authority and dominion on the earth (Genesis 1:26). When Adam sinned in the Garden of Eden, he turned the authority in the earth over to Satan (Luke 4:5, 6). As a result, Satan became the god of this world. In 2 Corinthians 4:4, Satan is referred to as the god (little "g") of this age (world). When Adam fell in the garden, Satan inherited that title from him.

God simply acknowledged that all that Job had was in Satan's power, but that is not the same as giving him permission to attack Job. Satan, as the god of this world, had the authority to come against Job.

Let us get some insight into the limited ability of Satan. Now we realize that Satan does have power. Luke 10:19 says that the child of God has been given the authority to trample over all the power of the enemy. Satan does have ability, but the believer has authority over all of Satan's power. Satan is not God's equivalent. His power is no match for God's power.

God not only has power—He is omnipotent or all-powerful. He has all power. Satan is not all-powerful. God is omniscient or all-knowing. Satan has limited knowledge, but not all knowledge. God also is omnipresent meaning that He is everywhere at one time. Satan is not omnipresent. He can only be one place at a time.

This is evident in Job 1:10 when Satan said to God, "'Have You not made a hedge around him, around his household, and around all that he has on every side?'" God, at one time, did have a hedge around him. But Job—not God, not Satan—pulled the hedge down. Obviously, Satan had not been around in a while because he had not noticed the hedge was down. If Satan were all-knowing, he would have known the hedge was down.

God's Nature Is to Bless People, Not Afflict Them

Job 3:25 gives us some insight as to how the hedge was pulled down in Job's life. This also tells us why evil things, bad things, and negative things happened to Job. God did not take things away from Job. God did not cause havoc and evil in Job's life. In fact, Satan asked God to put forth His hand and touch all that Job had. God refused to do it, but He told Satan that everything Job had was in his power. God refused to put a hand on Job because that is not God's nature. God's nature is to bless His people, not to afflict them.

Every Scripture in the Bible Is Truly Stated, but Every Scripture Is Not a Statement of Truth

In the New Testament, it says that the Old Testament scriptures were given for our admonition and for our learning. But many learn the wrong lesson. Have you ever been to a funeral service and somewhere in that service, the minister says these words from Job 1:21, "And he [Job] said, 'Naked I came from my mother's womb, And naked shall I return there. The LORD gave, and the LORD has taken away; Blessed be the name of the LORD.'"

Now it is true that Job said, "The LORD gave, and the LORD has taken away," or, "The LORD giveth and the LORD taketh away." However, that statement is not true. Here is something that is a principle of Bible interpretation. Knowing this important truth will enhance your understanding of the Bible: Every scripture is truly stated, but not every scripture in the Bible is a statement of truth.

Let me make another statement that may startle you at first, but just stay with me, and I will explain it. Hang onto your seat. All scripture is not inspired. Every scripture in the Bible is not inspired. I will show you from the Word of God that this is true. Let us read carefully from 2 Timothy 3:16.

> 2 Timothy 3:16
>
> 16 All Scripture is given by inspiration of God, and is profitable for doctrine, for reproof, for correction, for instruction in righteousness

It says that all scripture is given by inspiration of God and is profitable for doctrine, for reproof, for correction, and for instruction in righteousness. Notice, it says all scripture is given by inspiration of God. It does not say that all scripture is inspired. You may say, "Well, what is the difference?" I am going to tell you. Remember, I said that every scripture in the Bible is truly stated, but not every scripture is a statement of truth. The word *inspired* means "God-breathed."

Using Job's statement in Job 1:21 is a classic example. It is true that Job said, "The LORD gave, and the LORD has taken away," but what he said was not a statement of truth. It is true that the Lord gives, but it is not true that the Lord takes away. Therefore, it is unscriptural to use this in the context of a funeral service because God does not take life—He gives life. God does not take anyone out of this earth through death.

There were only three people in the Bible whom the Lord has taken. The first person was Enoch. The Bible says that Enoch walked with God, and God took him. However, God did not take him by death—God took him alive. The second person God took was Elijah. He too was taken alive. He was taken up by God in a whirlwind on a chariot.

The third person God took alive was the Lord Jesus Christ. After His resurrection, the Bible says in Acts 1:9 that a cloud received Him out of their (disciples) sight. So of the three people that the Bible says God took, He took all of them alive. Therefore, God does not take away. God does not take anyone out of here through death.

> John 10:10
>
> 10 "The thief does not come except to steal, and to kill, and to destroy.
> I have come that they may have life, and that they may have it more abundantly."

The Bible says, "The thief does not come except to steal, and to kill, and to destroy." But Jesus says, "I have come that they may have life, and that they may have it more abundantly." Jesus comes that we might have life. Satan is the thief. He is the one who steals, kills, and destroys—not God. Many people blame God for what the devil does so he gets off scot-free. He actually gets Christians to blame God for the things that he does.

1 Corinthians 15:26
26 The last enemy that will be destroyed is death.

The Bible says here that the last enemy that will be destroyed is death. That tells you that God cannot be the author of death. If that were the case then that would make God our enemy. Death is the last enemy that will be destroyed. Death does not have anything to do with God. Death is an enemy of God. Let us go back to 2 Timothy 3:16. It states, "All Scripture is given by inspiration of God."

All Scripture Is Not Inspired, but It Is Given by Inspiration of God

Let us say, for example, that company XYZ is having a board meeting, and its president makes a statement in the meeting, which is recorded by the secretary. The president states, "A man can get pregnant and have babies." The secretary writes that down just the way the president said it. One month later, the president calls the meeting into session and asks the secretary to read the minutes from the last meeting. And from those minutes she reads, "A man can get pregnant and have babies."

I want to ask you a question "Is that true?" What do you think...is it true or is it not? No, of course, it is not true! Although it is truly stated, it is not a statement of truth. Do you see the difference? The statement, "A man can get pregnant and have babies," is not a statement of truth; however, it was truly stated. The secretary recorded this statement exactly as the president had said it. In other words, it is recorded accurately, but it does not mean the statement itself is true.

Roadblocks to Healing

Now you can begin to understand what Job said in Job 1:21. He said, "The LORD gave, and the LORD has taken away." What Job said was not true. It was not a statement of truth, but it was truly stated. The author recorded it just the way the Holy Spirit wanted it written. It was written just the way the Holy Spirit wanted it recorded, but the statement made by Job was not a statement of truth. Job's words did not come from the Holy Spirit. Therefore, what Job said was not inspired, yet that scripture was given by inspiration of God.

Let me show you another example of this. Do you realize that the Bible says that there is no God? I want you to listen carefully because if you do not understand this point, it can make a difference between defeat and victory in your life. If you do not realize the difference between something that is truly stated and something that is a statement of truth, Satan can take scriptures in the Bible and whip you with them. Let us take a closer look at this scripture.

> Psalm 14:1
> 1 The fool has said in his heart, "THERE IS NO GOD." They are corrupt, They have done abominable works, there is none who does good. (Emphasis added)

Who said there was no God? The fool did. The fool says, "There is no God."

Well, this Psalm was recorded just the way the Holy Spirit wanted it recorded. It is truly stated, but the statement, "There is no God," is not a statement of truth. That statement made by the fool is not a statement of truth, but it was given by inspiration of God.

Job 1:21 says, "And he [Job] said: 'Naked I came from my mother's womb, and naked shall I return there. The LORD gave, and the LORD has taken away; Blessed be the name of the LORD.'"

The statement that the Lord gave and the Lord has taken away is not true.

We see that in Job, Chapter 1, God had refused to put His hand on Job. God did not cause havoc, destruction, sickness, and death in Job's life. It was Satan. When he came to Job, he found (because he is not all-knowing) that the hedge was down. Satan then began to cause destruction in Job's life. Now let us turn to Job 3:25 to find out how the hedge was pulled down in Job's life.

> Job 3:25
> 25 For the thing I greatly feared has come upon me,
> And what I dreaded has happened to me.

Job said, "For the thing I greatly feared has come upon me, and what I dreaded has happened to me."

> Job 3:25 (TLB)
> 25 What I always feared has happened to me.

This verse from the Living Bible says, "What I always feared has happened to me." Anything that you fear greatly may come upon you.

Here is a spiritual truth. Anything that you fear greatly may come upon you. The negative things, the evil things, the bad things, and the destructive things that occurred in Job's life happened because he greatly feared them. He dreaded them. Fear is a negative magnet that attracts negative things into your life. We need to follow the admonishment given to us in 2 Timothy 1:7.

> 2 Timothy 1:7
> 7 For God has not given us a spirit of fear, but of
> power and of love and of a sound mind.

"For God has not given us a spirit of fear, but of power and of love and of a sound mind." Fear is the opposite of faith. Faith is a spiritual force and so is fear. Faith attracts, and it is a magnet that attracts the blessings of God to your life. Fear is a negative force, and it is a magnet that attracts the things that belong to Satan into your life.

Anything that you fear greatly may come upon you, and that is what happened to Job. That is why those terrible things happened to Job. Destruction came. Now let us consider the latter part of Job's life.

Job Came Out of His Temporary Trouble

> Job 42:10
> 10 And the LORD restored Job's losses when he prayed for his friends. Indeed the LORD gave Job twice as much as he had before.

When Job got back in faith and prayed for his friends, the Lord turned Job's situation around and gave him twice as much as before.

> Job 42:12-17
> 12 Now the LORD blessed the latter days of Job more than his beginning; for he had fourteen thousand sheep, six thousand camels, one thousand yoke of oxen, and one thousand female donkeys.
> 13 He also had seven sons and three daughters.
> 14 And he called the name of the first Jemimah, the name of the second Keziah, and the name of the third Keren-Happuch.
> 15 In all the land were found no women so beautiful as the daughters of Job; and their father gave them an inheritance among their brothers.
> 16 After this Job lived one hundred and forty years, and saw his children and grandchildren for four generations.
> 17 SO JOB DIED, OLD AND FULL OF DAYS.
> (Emphasis added)

As you can see, Job was blessed with twice as much as he had before. The latter days of Job were better than his beginning. Keep in mind that the whole book of Job transpired over a period of nine months to one year. According to verse 17, Job died after living a long life full of days. So Job came out of his temporary trouble.

Let us remember that we are talking about roadblocks that hinder people from receiving their healing. Let us look at roadblock number two. And this is a big one.

Roadblock #2—Paul's Thorn in the Flesh

> 2 Corinthians 12:7-10
> 7 And lest I should be exalted above measure by the abundance of the revelations, a THORN IN THE FLESH was given to me, a MESSENGER of Satan to BUFFET me, lest I be exalted above measure.
> 8 Concerning this THING I pleaded with the Lord three times that it might depart from me.
> 9 And He said to me, "My grace is sufficient for you, for My strength is made perfect in weakness." Therefore most gladly I will rather boast in my infirmities, that the power of Christ may rest upon me.
> 10 Therefore I take pleasure in infirmities, in reproaches, in needs, in persecutions, in distresses, for Christ's sake. For when I am weak, then I am strong. (Emphasis added)

First of all, the thorn in the flesh was not sickness. I will prove that to you very clearly from the Word of God. You will be able to see it once these scriptures are revealed to you (it is very easy to understand).

Let us say, for instance, that the thorn in the flesh was sickness and that Paul had asked God three times to heal him; and each time God had refused. We would then have a contradiction in the Bible because this would be the first time that God had ever refused anyone who came to Him for healing.

In the ministry of the Lord Jesus Christ on the earth, no one who came to Him for healing was ever refused or turned down. And if God should refuse to heal Paul one time (much less three), that would make God a respecter of persons.

Acts 10:34
34 Then Peter opened his mouth and said: "In truth I perceive that God shows no partiality."

It says here in Acts 10:34 that "God shows no partiality." In other words, God is no respecter of persons. If God ever healed anyone, He will heal you because He is no respecter of persons. The *thorn in the flesh* is a figure of speech.

Now notice three things about Paul's thorn in the flesh. First of all, the Bible does not say that God gave Paul this thorn. Whatever it was, this passage never states that God gave it to him. Second, Paul did not say the thorn was sickness. And third, Paul tells us exactly what the thorn was. We are going to research the word *thorns* throughout the Old Testament, and we will see why the *thorn in the flesh* is not sickness or disease. The thorn in the flesh is a figure of speech.

Numbers 33:55
55 'But if you do not drive out the inhabitants of the land from before you, then it shall be that those whom you let remain shall be irritants in your eyes and thorns in your sides, and they shall harass you in the land where you dwell.'

This verse is part of the instructions God gave Israel on what to do when they conquered Canaan.

Notice the phrase *thorns in your sides*. The word *thorns* is not referring to an actual thorn that is literally in their side. He did not mean that the Canaanites would be planted into their side with their legs sticking out. This word is used figuratively or as a figure of speech, and it is used in reference to people.

The Bible uses the figure of speech much like we do today. For example, you hear people say, "That person is a pain in the neck." Well, they do not mean that this person is literally living in their neck. That phrase is a figure of speech.

Numbers 33:55 uses a second figure of speech. It says, "[the Canaanites] shall be irritants in your eyes." This does not mean that the Canaanites will literally be in their eyes as an irritant. It means that the Canaanites would be as annoying or irritating much like grains of sand would be to your eyes. So the phrases *irritants in your eyes* and *thorns in your sides* are used here figuratively.

Here is another passage that uses the word *thorns* in reference to people.

> Joshua 23:11-13
> 11 "Therefore take careful heed to yourselves, that you love the LORD your God.
> 12 "Or else, if indeed you do go back, and cling to the remnant of these nations—these that remain among you—and make marriages with them, and go in to them and they to you,
> 13 "know for certain that the LORD your God will no longer drive out these nations from before you. But they shall be snares and traps to you, and scourges on your sides and thorns in your eyes, until you perish from this good land which the LORD your God has given you."

In this passage, God is exhorting the children of Israel not to associate with their enemies. If they do, verse 13 says, "They shall be snares and traps to you, and scourges on your sides and thorns in your eyes." Notice the use of the word *thorns*. The phrase *thorns in your eyes* is used as a figure of speech, not as a literal thorn in their eyes. This passage uses the word *thorns* as an illustration to describe people.

> Judges 2:1-3
> 1 Then the Angel of the LORD came up from Gilgal to Bochim, and said: "I led you up from Egypt and brought you to the land of which I swore to your fathers; and I said, 'I will never break My covenant with you.

> 2 'And you shall make no covenant with the inhabitants of this land; you shall tear down their altars.' But you have not obeyed My voice. Why have you done this?
> 3 "Therefore I also said, 'I will not drive them out before you; but they shall be thorns in your side, and their gods shall be a snare to you.'"

Here again, we see the same thing. Verse 3 says, "I will not drive them out before you; but they shall be thorns in your side." *Thorns* is used here as a figure of speech to describe people or inhabitants of the land. Thorns are not used literally.

> 2 Samuel 23:6
> 6 But the sons of rebellion shall all be as thorns thrust away, Because they cannot be taken with hands.

This passage says, "But the sons of rebellion shall all be as thorns thrust away." Again, *thorns* is used to describe people—the sons of rebellion. It is used as a figure of speech, not as a literal thorn.

The Bible says, "By the mouth of two or three witnesses every word may be established" (Matthew 18:16). We have referred to four passages of scripture that clearly uses the word *thorns* to describe personalities, not things. Thorns are not used literally, but figuratively.

Now let us follow this train of thought to 2 Corinthians, Chapter 12, concerning Paul's thorn in the flesh. Based on the pattern that we see concerning the word *thorn* in the Bible, we can conclude that Paul's thorn in the flesh was not a literal thorn. The phrase *thorn in the flesh* was used as a figure of speech to describe people and not things. Paul's thorn in the flesh was not literal. It was not a thing. It was a personality. The word *thorn* in the Bible was never used to describe sickness or disease.

Let us move on to another point. Let us look at the word *messenger* in 2 Corinthians 12:7. Paul said that the thorn was "a messenger of Satan to buffet me." The Greek word translated as messenger is *angelos* and is found 186 times in the New Testament. In 179 times out of the 186, this word is translated as angel or angels. And in every case (all 186 times), this word is used in reference to a being, not to a thing.

If we use angel instead of messenger in verse 7, we see that *the thorn in the flesh* was actually an angel of Satan. The definition of the Greek word *angelos* is "a person whom one sends to another person"—never a sickness or a disease. It is interesting that the word *angelos* is actually a being because that is consistent with what we found out about thorns in the previous passages.

Let us now look at the word *buffet*. Verse 7 says, "A thorn in the flesh was given to me, a messenger of Satan to BUFFET me." The word *buffet* means repeated blows or blow after blow. For example, the word *buffet* can be used in reference to waves of the sea that buffet against a ship. Buffet does not mean something that comes on someone or something and remains. Instead, it describes repeated, ongoing blows. Richard Frances Weymouth's translation of verse 7 says, "Satan's angel dealing blow after blow."

In verse 8, Paul goes on to say, "Concerning this THING I pleaded with the Lord three times that IT might depart from me." (Emphasis added) The words *thing* and *it* in this verse seem to contradict what we have learned thus far regarding the thorn in the flesh. We have already pointed out that these words are used in reference to personalities or beings, not to things. But I submit to you that this is a mistranslation.

Again, I refer to Weymouth's translation of this verse, "As for this, three times have I besought the Lord to rid me of HIM." Weymouth uses the personal pronoun him. This translation verifies the fact that this thorn was a being, not a sickness. You would not use the word him to describe a sickness because a sickness is not a person. It is a thing.

Let us take another look at Weymouth's translation of verse 8. "As for this, three times have I besought the Lord to rid me of him." Now let us go a little bit further. In this verse, Paul asked the Lord three times to rid him of this thorn (this being). God's response to Paul was that His grace was sufficient.

God's grace was sufficient, not insufficient. When you think of the word *sufficient*, you think of something being enough. So another way of saying "My grace is sufficient" is "My grace is good enough." What

God has already supplied Paul was good enough to face this thorn that he was dealing with. God has supplied Paul with His grace.

When we understand what is God's grace, we will be able to understand the massive, overcoming resources that were available to Paul. By definition, God's grace is unmerited favor. When you look at it from that standpoint, God is not implying that Paul is defenseless against the thorn. Rather, God is telling Paul that His unmerited favor is sufficient for him to overcome anything he faces, including this thorn. God's favor on your life will get you through anything.

Paul's thorn was a demon spirit sent from Satan to stir up trouble for Paul.

Paul's thorn in the flesh was not sickness or disease or a thing. Paul's thorn in the flesh was a demon spirit sent from Satan to stir up trouble for Paul wherever he went. The suffering that Paul went through in his life was not sickness and disease, but persecution. As children of God, all of us will suffer persecution. But the good news is that God will deliver us out of all persecution.

> 2 Timothy 3:10-12
> 10 But you have carefully followed my doctrine, manner of life, purpose, faith, longsuffering, love, perseverance,
> 11 PERSECUTIONS, afflictions, which happened to me at Antioch, at Iconium, at Lystra —what PERSECUTIONS I endured. And out of them all THE LORD DELIVERED ME.
> 12 Yes, and all who desire to live godly in Christ Jesus will suffer PERSECUTION. (Emphasis added)

In verse 11, Paul talks about the persecutions and afflictions that came against him. He endured them, and out of all of them, the Lord delivered him. Then he says in verse 12, "All who desire to live godly in Christ Jesus will suffer persecution." As you live for God, you will be persecuted. But out of them all, the Lord will deliver you when you put your trust in Him. His grace is sufficient to cause you to overcome every affliction and persecution that comes your way.

Now that we understand that the thorn in the flesh is a demon spirit, let me tell you why God could not take the thorn away. The reason God could not take the thorn or the evil spirit away from Paul is because the demons and evil spirits have a right to be here.

Demons and evil spirits are messengers or angels of Satan. They have a right to be here because Adam turned the authority in the earth over to Satan when he sinned in the Garden of Eden.

We can see from Jesus' temptation in the wilderness that Satan has authority over all the kingdoms of the world. Luke 4:5 says, "Then the devil, taking Him [Jesus] up on a high mountain, showed Him all the KINGDOMS OF THE WORLD in a moment of time." (Emphasis added)

The devil said to Jesus in verse 6, "All this AUTHORITY I will give You, and their glory." (Emphasis added) Now the authority that he was talking about was the authority of the kingdoms of the world. Continuing in verse 6, Satan said, "For this has been delivered to me, and I give it to whomever I wish."

Now Satan could not have been lying here when he said that the authority of the kingdoms of the world have been delivered to him. The reason for that is because the Bible calls this experience a temptation. For a temptation to be valid, you must have the ability to yield. What makes a temptation a temptation is your ability to yield. Therefore, Jesus must have had the ability to yield. The kingdoms of the world had to be Satan's to offer; else it would not have been a legitimate temptation for Jesus.

The point I am making is this: Satan had the kingdoms of the world to offer to Jesus because Adam had delivered it to him. This occurred the moment that Adam ate of the tree of the knowledge of good and evil in the Garden of Eden. And Satan has been here ever since as the "god of this world." Satan has a temporary lease on the earth. The Bible says, "The devil walks about like a roaring lion, seeking whom he may devour" (1 Peter 5:8).

> Matthew 8:28, 29
> 28 When He had come to the other side, to the country of the Gergesenes, there met Him two demon-possessed men, coming out of the tombs,

exceedingly fierce, so that no one could pass that way.
29 And suddenly they cried out, saying, "What have we to do with You, Jesus, You Son of God? Have You come here to torment us before the time?"

In these verses, two demon-possessed men came to Jesus. The demons spoke through the men and cried out to Jesus, saying, "What have we to do with You, Jesus, You Son of God? Have You come here to torment us before the time?"

Notice the words "before the time." This reveals to us that the demons know that there is a time when they will be removed from the earth. Even though Satan is the god of this world, there will come a time when Satan will be evicted. Satan only has a temporary lease on the earth because Christ will one day return to rule and reign on the new earth. So there will come a time when Satan will be evicted. But until then, he and his demons have a right to be here. God will not remove him from the earth.

It is like a person who rents an apartment. He does not own the apartment, but he has a right to put furniture in the apartment and arrange the apartment any way he pleases. The owner cannot just barge in anytime he wants, sits down in his living room, and watch TV. He has to abide by the rules of the contract. Satan has a temporary lease on the earth, and he has a right to be here until his lease runs out. Why do you think that this world is in such a mess? Certainly, you do not think God is responsible for all the inequalities and injustices that exist in the world. No, Satan is responsible. And God will not do anything about it until Satan's lease is up.

These demons asked Jesus, "Have You come here to torment us before the time?" They knew that until the time comes for them to be evicted from the earth, they have a right to be here. They have a right to roam to and fro throughout the earth. Therefore, the reason why God could not remove the *thorn in the flesh* or the demon spirit from Paul was because they have a right to be here.

Let us take a look at Paul's persecutions and sufferings. In 2 Corinthians 12:10 Paul says, "Therefore I take pleasure in infirmities, in reproaches, in needs, in persecutions, in distresses, for Christ's sake.

For when I am weak, then I am strong." If Paul's thorn was sickness, then why does he not mention it in describing the various things that he went through? He mentions infirmities, reproaches, needs, persecutions, and distresses. Sickness is not mentioned.

At the end of verse 10, it says, "For when I am weak, then I am strong." What Paul is saying is that he recognizes he cannot withstand the onslaught of Satan in his own ability. Remember we pointed out to you that the thorn in the flesh was a messenger of Satan or an angel of Satan that was sent to stir up trouble for Paul wherever he went.

Paul says that when he is weak (from a natural standpoint), then he is strong (in the Lord). Paul states in Ephesians 6:10, "Be strong in the Lord and in the power of His might." Joel 3:10 says, "Let the weak say, 'I am strong.'" When you are weak, do not confess that you are weak. Confess that you are strong in the Lord and in the power of His might, and then the power and strength of God will kick in and enable you to overcome.

Sometimes you are weak from a natural standpoint, and the flesh does get weary. But praise God, we have the Holy Spirit on the inside of us, who gives us power that is available to us whenever we need it. The Comforter, the Holy Spirit, abides in us forever. Acts 1:8 says, "But you shall receive power when the Holy Spirit has come upon you."

> Romans 8:11
> 11 But if the Spirit of Him who raised Jesus from the dead dwells in you, He who raised Christ from the dead will also give life to your mortal bodies through His Spirit who dwells in you.

It says that the Spirit of Him (God) who raised Jesus from the dead is on the inside of you, and (God) will give life to your mortal bodies by His Spirit who dwells in you.

> 2 Corinthians 12:9
> 9 And He said to me, "My grace is sufficient for you, for MY STRENGTH IS MADE PERFECT IN WEAKNESS." Therefore most gladly I will rather

boast in my infirmities, that the power of Christ may rest upon me. (Emphasis added)

Jesus said to Paul, "My grace is sufficient for you, for My strength is made perfect in weakness." This tells us here that Paul was not defeated. For Christ's strength to be made perfect in his weakness, Paul could not have remained weak. Paul was a partaker of Christ's strength, which removed the weakness.

2 Corinthians 11:22-28
22 Are they Hebrews? So am I. Are they Israelites? So am I. Are they the seed of Abraham? So am I.
23 Are they ministers of Christ? —I speak as a fool—I am more: in labors more abundant, in stripes above measure, in prisons more frequently, in deaths often.
24 From the Jews five times I received forty stripes minus one.
25 Three times I was beaten with rods; once I was stoned; three times I was shipwrecked; a night and a day I have been in the deep;
26 in journeys often, in perils of waters, in
perils of robbers, in perils of my own countrymen, in perils of the Gentiles, in perils in the city, in perils in the wilderness, in perils in the sea, in perils among false brethren;
27 in weariness and toil, in sleeplessness often, in hunger and thirst, in fastings often, in cold and nakedness—
28 besides the other things, what comes upon me daily: my deep concern for all the churches.

Let us look at scriptures throughout the New Testament and find out from Paul what he went through rather than take someone else's word that Paul went through sickness. If Paul's thorn in the flesh was sickness, then we ought to be able to hear Paul say that it was. But it is interesting to note that Paul does not mention sickness or disease as a part of his suffering.

Again in 2 Corinthians 12:10, Paul mentions what he went through for Christ's sake: infirmities, reproaches, needs, persecutions, and distresses.

In 2 Corinthians 11:23-28, Paul describes his suffering in more detail. He states that he was more abundant in labors, in stripes above measure, in prisons more frequently, and in deaths often. He received thirty-nine stripes five times from the Jews. He was beaten with rods three times; he was once stoned; he was shipwrecked three times; and he has been in the deep a night and a day. He was in journeys often, in perils of waters, in perils of robbers, in perils of his own countrymen, in perils of the Gentiles, in perils in the city, in perils in the wilderness, in perils in the sea, and in perils among false brethren. He was in weariness and toil, in sleeplessness often, in hunger and thirst, in fastings often, and in cold and nakedness. However, in verse 29, Paul goes on to say, "Who is weak, and I am not weak?" So that ought to tell you that he was not a sick man.

In verse 23, Paul mentions that he was "in labors more abundant." Paul was a man who traveled extensively, established many churches, and was responsible for over half of the New Testament. Now if Paul was a sick man all of his life like some people say, then we all need to pray that we get the same sickness so that we can accomplish half of the things that he did in his ministry!

> 1 Corinthians 4:11
> 11 To the present hour we both hunger and thirst, and we are poorly clothed, and BEATEN, and homeless. (Emphasis added)

The Greek word translated *beaten* is the same Greek word translated *buffeted* in 2 Corinthians 12:7. Since the word *beaten* is not used in reference to sickness or disease, why should we think that the word *buffet* has to do with sickness or disease?

2 Corinthians 6:4-10
4 But in all things we commend ourselves as ministers of God: in much patience, in tribulations, in needs, in distresses,
5 in stripes, in imprisonments, in tumults, in labors, in sleeplessness, in fastings;
6 by purity, by knowledge, by longsuffering, by kindness, by the Holy Spirit, by sincere love,
7 by the word of truth, by the power of God, by the armor of righteousness on the right hand and on the left,
8 by honor and dishonor, by evil report and good report; as deceivers, and yet true;
9 as unknown, and yet well known; as dying, and behold we live; as chastened, and yet not killed;
10 as sorrowful, yet always rejoicing; as poor, yet making many rich; as having nothing, and yet possessing all things.

2 Corinthians 4:8-10
8 We are hard-pressed on every side, yet not crushed; we are perplexed, but not in despair;
9 persecuted, but not forsaken; struck down, but not destroyed—
10 always carrying about in the body the dying of the Lord Jesus, that the life of Jesus also may be manifested in our body.

1 Corinthians 4:11-13
11 To the present hour we both hunger and thirst, and we are poorly clothed, and beaten, and homeless.
12 And we labor, working with our own hands. Being reviled, we bless; being persecuted, we endure;

13 being defamed, we entreat. We have been made as
the filth of the world, the offscourging of all things
until now.

Here Paul lists some other things that he suffered including, stripes, imprisonments, tumults, labors, sleeplessness, fastings, dishonor, evil reports, deceivers, dying, chastenings, being hard-pressed, persecutions, and being struck down. I like what Philip's translation says: "Paul was knocked down, but he was not knocked out."

At times, Paul was sorrowful, yet he always rejoiced; there were times he was poor, yet he made many rich; and there were times he had nothing, yet he possessed all things. There were times he felt both hunger and thirst. There were times He was poorly clothed, beaten, homeless, reviled, persecuted, defamed, made as the filth of the world, and made as the offscourging of all things until now. As we listen to the Apostle Paul describe all of the things that he went through, I want you to notice that he does not mention sickness as one of the things he suffered.

Romans 15:29
29 But I know that when I come to you, I shall come
in the fullness of the blessing of the gospel of Christ.

We have already shown you from scripture that healing is a part of the gospel. Paul tells the church at Rome, "But I know that when I come to you, I shall come in the fullness of the blessing of the gospel of Christ" (Romans 15:29).

Healing is one of the blessings of the gospel of Christ. Again, I call your attention to Psalm 103 verses 1 thru 3. It says, "Bless the LORD, O my soul; and all that is within me, bless His Holy name! Bless the LORD, O my soul, and forget not all His benefits: who forgives all your iniquities, who HEALS all your diseases." (Emphasis added)

Healing is one of the benefits of Calvary. Healing is one of the great benefits of the gospel of Christ. Not only do we have our sins forgiven, but we also have all of our diseases healed. First Peter 2:24 says, "By whose stripes you were healed." Matthew 8:17 says, "He Himself...bore our sicknesses."

Paul says, "But I know that when I come to you, I shall come in the fullness of the blessing of the gospel of Christ" (Romans 15:29). And one of the blessings of the gospel is healing. If Paul was as sick as some people would like us to believe, how could he come in the fullness of the blessing of the gospel of Christ? When he came in the fullness of the blessing of the gospel of Christ, he came fully healed.

Here is something else we need to look at. If Paul's thorn in the flesh was sickness, how could he encourage others to receive their healing?

> Acts 19:11,12
> 11 Now God worked unusual miracles by the hands of Paul,
> 12 so that even handkerchiefs or aprons were brought from his body to the sick, and the diseases left them and the evil spirits went out of them.

Acts 19:12 says, "So that even handkerchiefs or aprons were brought from his body to the sick, and the diseases left them and the evil spirits went out of them." So obviously, Paul laid hands on handkerchiefs and aprons. When the cloths were laid on the sick people, they were healed. And those who had demon spirits were delivered from them.

Do you think sick people would want cloths that came from Paul's body if he was a sickly man? I do not think so. Again, Acts 19:12 says, "Handkerchiefs or aprons were brought from his [Paul's] body to the sick, and the diseases left them and the evil spirits went out of them."

I am convinced that those handkerchiefs and aprons did not come from a sick man's body. If Paul was so sick, do you think the people that he ministered to would have had faith for the special miracles that Paul worked among them? Do you think they would have been encouraged to come and to receive their miracle? I do not think so.

Romans 15:18, 19
18 For I will not dare to speak of any of those things which Christ has not accomplished through me, in word and deed, to make the Gentiles obedient
19 in mighty signs and wonders, by the power of the Spirit of God, so that from Jerusalem and round about to Illyricum I have fully preached the gospel of Christ.

It is amazing how Paul, who was supposedly so sick—who had this thorn in the flesh of sickness, which God refused to heal—could accomplish such great things. He made the Gentiles obedient by word and deed through mighty signs and wonders, by the power of the Spirit of God. I do not think this is describing a sick man.

2 Corinthians 11:23
23 Are they ministers of Christ? —I speak as a fool—I am more: IN LABORS MORE ABUNDANT, in stripes above measure, in prisons more frequently, in deaths often. (Emphasis added)

I ask you, could Paul labor more abundantly if he was sickly due to a thorn in the flesh? I think not.

2 Timothy 3:17
17 that the man of God may be complete, THOROUGHLY EQUIPPED FOR EVERY GOOD WORK. (Emphasis added)

Titus 2:11-14
11 For the grace of God that brings salvation has appeared to all men,
12 teaching us that, denying ungodliness and worldly lusts, we should live soberly, righteously, and godly in the present age,

13 looking for the blessed hope and glorious appearing of our great God and Saviour Jesus Christ, 14 who gave Himself for us, that He might redeem us from every lawless deed and purify for Himself His own special people, ZEALOUS FOR GOOD WORKS. (Emphasis added)

Titus 3:8
8 This is a faithful saying, and these things I want you to affirm constantly, that those who have believed in God should be CAREFUL TO MAINTAIN GOOD WORKS. These things are good and profitable to men. (Emphasis added)

Hebrews 13:20, 21
20 Now may the God of peace who brought up our Lord Jesus from the dead, that great Shepherd of the sheep, through the blood of the everlasting covenant, 21 make you COMPLETE IN EVERY GOOD WORK TO DO HIS WILL, working in you what is well pleasing in His sight, through Jesus Christ, to whom be glory forever and ever. Amen. (Emphasis added)

It was Paul who wrote that the Christian should be thoroughly equipped for every good work, zealous for good works, careful to maintain good works, and complete in every good work to do His will. How can we do those things if we are overcome with sickness and disease? You can do much more for God when you are well than when you are sick.

2 Timothy 4:7
7 I have fought the good fight, I have finished the race, I have kept the faith.

We see here that Paul finished his course. He kept the faith. Sickness and disease keep many people from living out their full life and finishing their course. Yet, Paul finished his course. He fought the good fight and kept the faith. Some well-meaning Christians are going to the graves with their course half run because of illness.

Roadblock #3 - The Man Born Blind

> John 9:1-7
> 1 Now as Jesus passed by, He saw a man who was blind from birth.
> 2 And His disciples asked Him, saying, "Rabbi, who sinned, this man or his parents, that he was born blind?"
> 3 Jesus answered, "Neither this man nor his parents sinned, but that the works of God should be revealed in him.
> 4 "I must work the works of Him who sent Me while it is day; the night is coming when no one can work.
> 5 "As long as I am in the world, I am the light of the world."
> 6 When He had said these things, He spat on the ground and made clay with the saliva; and He anointed the eyes of the blind man with the clay.
> 7 And He said to him, "Go, wash in the pool of Siloam" (which is translated, Sent). So he went and washed, and came back seeing.

In verse 2, the disciples wanted to ascertain the reason why the man was born blind. So they asked, "Who sinned, the man or his parents, that he was born blind?" They obviously believed that it was possible for a child to sin in his mother's womb.

It is interesting to note that the disciples did not ask, "Did God make him blind?" They knew that God did not cause sickness and disease. In answering their question as to who had sinned, Jesus could have answered: the man, his parents, or neither. Pay particular attention to Verse 3 because I am going to change, for the sake of clarity, the punctuation in this verse. By doing this, I will not do any injustice to the scripture.

You see the punctuation that exists in the modern translations is not inspired. The text is inspired but not the punctuation. Punctuation marks (such as commas, periods, colons, and semi-colons), small case letters, chapter divisions, and verse distinctions were all added by the translators to render clarity. But in this case, it rendered confusion.

The punctuation as used in John 9, verses 3 and 4, obscures the true meaning of this passage. In verse 3, Jesus answered, "Neither this man nor his parents sinned, but that the works of God should be revealed in him."

The way this is punctuated, it appears as though the man's blindness was the work of God. But Jesus cannot be saying that because it would not fit the teaching in God's Word on the subject of healing. Acts 10:38 and Luke 13:11-16 shows us clearly that sickness and disease is not a work of God but a work of Satan. Acts 10:38 says, "Who [Jesus] went about doing good and healing all who were oppressed by the devil."

If you change the punctuation in John 9 verses 3 and 4, you can clearly see what Jesus is saying. Let us change the punctuation and see what a difference it makes. The disciples asked Jesus, "Who sinned, this man or his parents, that he was born blind?" We can change verse 3 to say, "Jesus answered, 'Neither this man nor his parents sinned. [period]'" Now they have the answer to their question.

Continuing with these verses, let us change it to say, "But that the works of God should be revealed in him, I must work the works of Him who sent Me while it is day; the night is coming when no one can work."

Can you see how that changes the meaning of these passages? By reading it this way, it reveals that the works of God had nothing to do with making this man blind. The works of God was healing the man of his blindness. Jesus said, "But that the works of God should be revealed in him, I must work the work." So the works of God was not manifest in this man while he was still blind. The works of God was the eventual healing of the man.

In verses 6 and 7, it says, "He [Jesus] spat on the ground and made clay with the saliva; and He anointed the eyes of the blind man with the clay. And He said to him, 'Go, wash in the pool of Siloam' (which is translated *sent*). So he went, washed, and came back seeing."

When Jesus spoke of the works of God that, "should be revealed in him", Jesus was referring to the healing of the blind man. You cannot use this passage to teach that sickness is a work of God. Meditation and study of this passage clearly reveal that the works of God consisted of healing the man of his blindness, not in causing the man's blindness.

Roadblock #4 - Paul's Infirmity

> Galatians 4:13, 14
> 13 You know that because of PHYSICAL INFIRMITY I preached the gospel to you at the first. (Emphasis added)
> 14 And my trial which was in my flesh you did not despise or reject, but you received me as an angel of God, even as Christ Jesus.

The Greek word translated *infirmity* also means sickness. However, there is no evidence that this infirmity was an illness. But even if it was, you cannot build a doctrine on one verse. You cannot use this isolated verse to say that Paul was a sick man all of his life. This passage does not give us enough scriptural evidence to prove that Paul was sick because it cannot be substantiated by any other verse in the Bible.

A possible explanation of this verse is found in Acts 14 verses 19 and 20.

> Acts 14:19, 20
> 19 Then Jews from Antioch and Iconium came there; and having persuaded the multitudes, they stoned Paul and dragged him out of the city, supposing him to be dead.

> 20 However, when the disciples gathered around him, he rose up and went into the city. And the next day he departed with Barnabas to Derbe.

Paul's weakness may have taken place after he was stoned. But notice in Acts 14, verse 20, he rose up after being stoned, came into the city, and departed to Derby the next day. Paul was nearly stoned to death, yet he preached the very next day in another city. Even stoning did not stop Paul from preaching the gospel. That does not sound like a sick man to me.

Roadblock #5 - Timothy's Frequent Infirmities

> 1 Timothy 5:23
> 23 No longer drink only water, but use a little wine for your stomach's sake and your FREQUENT INFIRMITIES. (Emphasis added)

We do not know why Timothy was sick. The implication here is that Timothy's infirmities were some sort of sickness. This verse is not telling us that it is God's will for us to be sick. It is simply saying that Timothy was frequently ill. But we do not know the reason why.

Roadblock #6 - Paul Left Trophimus Sick

> 2 Timothy 4:20
> 20 Erastus stayed in Corinth, but TROPHIMUS I HAVE LEFT IN MILETUS SICK. (Emphasis added)

When Paul departed, he left Trophimus sick at Miletus. In Acts, Chapter 28, Paul did not leave the people who came to him sick on the Island of Mileta. Why did he leave Trophimus sick? I do not know; the scripture does not say. There are people in the body of Christ who are sick and go to the doctor. That does not make them any less of a Christian than somebody who is healed. But I am teaching God's best concerning healing. Not everyone attains to God's best and that does not make them any less of a Christian. Teaching what the Bible says concerning healing is to point people to God's best, not to put God's people in condemnation.

Some are people who are sick because they disobey natural laws such as going outside wet without a coat on when it is 20 degrees below zero. That does not have anything to do with God's will—that is being unwise.

> 1 Corinthians 11:30
> 30 For this reason many are weak and sick among you, and many sleep.

Discern means "to see or understand." One reason some people are left sick or remain sick is because they do not understand the Lord's body. This is why some people are sick and others even die. I will deal with this in more detail later in the book.

Roadblock #7 - Epaphroditus' Sickness

> Philippians 2:26, 27
> 26 since he was longing for you all, and was distressed because you had hear that he was sick.
> 27 For indeed he was sick almost unto death; but God had mercy on him, and not only on him but on me also, lest I should have sorrow upon sorrow.

If you go on reading this passage, you will find that Epaphroditus was sick because he ignored the limitations of his body.

> Philippians 2:30
> 30 because for the work of Christ he came close to death, not regarding his life, to supply what was lacking in your service toward me.

Epaphroditus was sick because of overwork. You can overwork yourself even in the work of the ministry. Overwork can cause sickness in your body.

But understand this: the fact that there were people in the Bible who were sick does not mean that it was God's will for them to be that way.

We showed you from the Word of God that God established a covenant of healing in the Old Testament. God reveals Himself as our Healer through one of His redemptive names, Jehovah Rapha, in Exodus 15:26. Jehovah Rapha means "I am the Lord who heals you."

In Exodus 23:25, God said, "I will take sickness away from the midst of you." As long as Israel walked in line with God's laws, His commandments, His precepts, and His statutes, God was there for them in every area of their life, including healing.

In the ministry of Jesus, we showed you from the four gospels (Matthew, Mark, Luke, and John) how Jesus healed the multitudes and how He was the will of God in action. Jesus demonstrated to us God's attitude towards sickness and disease.

Jesus never saw the Father turn anybody down who came to Him for healing. And since Jesus only did what He saw His Father do, He never turned anybody down who came to Him for healing either. There is no record in the Bible from Genesis to Revelation of God ever refusing anyone who came to Him seeking healing.

Now here is my point: if God was the Healer under the Old Covenant, and if He was the Healer during the ministry of Jesus, then He is still our Healer today. Let me show you why.

> Hebrews 8:6
> 5 But now He has obtained A MORE EXCELLENT MINISTRY, inasmuch as He is also Mediator of a better covenant, which was established on better promises. (Emphasis added)

Here it says Jesus has obtained a more excellent ministry. When Jesus walked the earth, we know that He spent a great deal of His ministry healing the sick. So if He has a more excellent ministry now —where He is at the right hand of the Father, where He ever lives to make intercession for us—His ministry would have to include the healing of the sick. If it did not, it would not be more excellent.

This verse goes on to say, "Jesus is also Mediator of a better covenant, which was established on better promises." So referring to this New Covenant that we live in today—the age of grace, the age of the Holy Spirit—this covenant (in order to be better than the old) must at least have everything that the Old Covenant had and more for it to be better.

The Old Covenant was a covenant of healing. If the New Covenant did not have healing, it would not be better, would it? So if the Old Covenant had healing, then the New Covenant has to have healing because it is a better covenant established upon better promises.

> James 1:17
> 17 Every GOOD GIFT and every perfect gift is from above, and comes down from the Father of lights, with whom there is no variation or shadow of turning. (Emphasis added)

Every good gift, which includes healing, and every perfect gift is from above. Bad things do not come from God, only good gifts. "Every good gift and every perfect gift is from above, and comes down from the Father of lights, with whom there is no variation or shadow of turning."

This verse says, "There is no variation [with God] or shadow of turning." In other words, God does not change even slightly. There is no shadow of turning with God; He does not change. So since God does not change, He must still be our Healer today. In Exodus 15:26, He reveals Himself as Jehovah Rapha, the Lord who heals us. If He was the Lord who healed us then, He must still be the Lord who heals us now because He does not change.

> Malachi 3:6
> 6 "For I am the LORD, I do not change; Therefore you are not consumed,
> O sons of Jacob."

Here it says, "For I am the LORD, I do not change." God does not change. Concerning the phrase "I do not change," the Companion Bible says this, "Not in Himself, nor in His purpose, to change His dealings on the condition stated."[2]

God does not change in Himself. God does not change in His purpose nor does He change in His dealings on the condition stated. In other words, when God states His position concerning healing, it is established and He does not change it. If He was ever our Healer, He always will be our Healer.

> Hebrews 13:8
> 8 Jesus Christ is the same yesterday, today, and forever.

"Jesus Christ is the same yesterday, today, and forever." One Bible scholar says the same means "He is the same identical person in every respect". Since Jesus Christ healed in His earthly ministry, He must still be in the healing business today; else He would not be the same. Jesus Christ is the identical person in every respect—yesterday, today, and forever. If He healed yesterday, He heals today, and He will always heal. Praise God forevermore!

---

[2] Companion Bible, Malachi 3:6, Bullinger. 1901-Haywood. 2005 (Public Domain).

7.
Is God Glorified Through Sickness?

God does not put sickness on people. Sickness does not come from God. So if sickness does not come from God, who does it come from? It comes from the devil. In John, Chapter 9, we showed you it was not the work of God that the man was born blind. The work of God was to heal the blind man. In Acts 10:38 and Luke 13:11-16, we saw that sickness was satanic oppression.

Is God glorified through sickness? NO! Now in sickness, you can praise God because the Bible says, "In everything give thanks." Even when you are sick, you can thank God but not for the sickness. You should thank God for healing while you are sick. Now you can thank God in sickness, and you can give God glory in sickness. But when I ask, "Is God glorified through sickness?" I am asking whether God gets the glory through people because of their sickness?

Some people say, "Well, it was not until that person was sick and in the hospital that they heard God." They could have heard God before they became sick. And sure, they may not have heard God until they went into the hospital. They may have turned to God because they could not go out and party all night as they did before. They are lying on the hospital bed with tubes running through their body as they stare at the ceiling. They cannot run around and do their own thing. And sure, they hear God but only because God can now get their attention.

God does not use bad things to get people to repent. Some say, "Well, it was not until so-and-so was in jail and was ministered to before they began living for God. It was not until they were in jail that they were saved.

Was it God's will that they were sent to jail? NO! God does not cause bad things to happen to get people to repent. But what God does is to cause good things to happen in spite of a bad situation. However, He does not commission bad things to happen.

God does not put bad things on people to get them to repent. However, some people tell us that God causes negative things and negative circumstances to happen to get people to repent. They claim He gets glory from them being sick. They say, "Yes, God's got a purpose in that. God saw fit to call that person home. God took that person's life because He knew that seventeen people would get saved at the funeral." All of that is human reasoning—it is not in the Bible.

Suppose if that person had lived thirty or forty or more years. They could have gotten fifty people saved themselves. God does not cause bad things to get people to repent. The Word of God says so.

> Romans 2:1-4
> 1 Therefore you are inexcusable, O man, whoever you are who judge, for in whatever you judge another you condemn yourself; for you who judge practice the same things.
> 2 But we know that the judgment of God is according to truth against those who practice such things.
> 3 And do you think this, O man, you who judge those practicing such things, and doing the same, that you will escape the judgment of God?
> 4 Or do you despise the riches of His goodness, forbearance, and long-suffering, not knowing that THE GOODNESS OF GOD LEADS YOU TO REPENTANCE? (Emphasis added)

It is the goodness of God that leads people to repentance. God intends for the preaching of the Word to get people to repent. People will be led to repent if you tell them how good God is. Tell them about God's love. Tell them about God's grace. Tell them about God's mercy. Tell them that Jesus Christ died for their sins. Tell them they can be born again and live an abundant, prosperous, and victorious life. Tell them they can be redeemed from poverty, sickness, and spiritual death!

That is good news. It is the goodness of God, not bad things or condemnation that leads people to repentance. It is God's will that His goodness leads you to repentance.

Is God glorified through sickness? Let us find scripture to see how and when God gets the glory.

> Luke 13:11-13
> 11 And behold, there was a woman who had a spirit of infirmity eighteen years, and was bent over and could in no way raise herself up.
> 12 But when Jesus saw her, He called her to Him and said to her, "Woman, you are loosed from your infirmity."
> 13 And He laid His hands on her, and immediately she was made straight, and GLORIFIED GOD. (Emphasis added)

We did not hear any praising or worshipping going on while she was sick. When she was healed, she gave God glory! It was not until she was made straight that God got the glory, not when she was bound.

> Matthew 9:1-8
> 1 So He got into a boat, crossed over, and came to His own city.
> 2 Then behold, they brought to Him a paralytic lying on a bed. When Jesus saw their faith, He said to the paralytic, "Son, be of good cheer; your sins are forgiven you."
> 3 And at once some of the scribes said within themselves, "This Man blasphemes!"
> 4 But Jesus, knowing their thoughts, said, "Why do you think evil in your hearts?
> 5 "For which is easier, to say, 'Your sins are forgiven you,' or to say, 'Arise and walk'?

6 "But that you may know that the Son of Man has power on earth to forgive sins"—then He said to the paralytic, "Arise, take up your bed, and go to your house."
7 And he arose and departed to his house.
8 Now when the multitudes saw it, they marveled and GLORIFIED GOD, who had given such power to men. (Emphasis added)

They glorified God because the man was healed. God received the glory when this man was made whole. Notice, while the man was bound with paralysis, no mention was made of anyone glorifying God.

Matthew 15:29-31
29 Jesus departed from there, skirted the Sea of Galilee, and went up on the mountain and sat down there.
30 Then great multitudes came to Him, having with them the lame, blind, mute, maimed, and many others; and they laid them down at Jesus' feet, and He healed them.
31 So the multitude marveled when they saw the mute speaking, the maimed made whole, the lame walking, and the blind seeing; and THEY GLORIFIED THE GOD OF ISREAL. (Emphasis added)

There was not any praising, there was not any worshipping, and there was not any glorifying of God when they were bound with disease. But notice they glorified God when they were healed.

Is God Glorified Through Sickness?

> Luke 7:11-16
>
> 11 Now it happened, the day after, that He went into a city called Nain; and many of His disciples went with Him, and a large crowd.
>
> 12 And when He came near the gate of the city, behold, a dead man was being carried out, the only son of his mother;
>
> and she was a widow. And a large crowd from the city was with her.
>
> 13 When the Lord saw her, He had compassion on her and said to her, "Do not weep."
>
> 14 Then He came and touched the open coffin, and those who carried him stood still. And He said, "Young man, I say to you, arise."
>
> 15 So he who was dead sat up and began to speak. And He presented him to his mother.
>
> 16 Then fear came upon all, and THEY GLORIFIED GOD, saying, "A great prophet has risen up among us"; and, "God has visited His people." (Emphasis added)

They glorified God because the dead were raised! There is no mention of any praising or worshipping going on during the funeral procession. Many people talk about God getting the glory of people being sick. But that is unscriptural. God gets the glory when people are healed.

> Luke 17:11-18
>
> 11 Now it happened as He went to Jerusalem that He passed through the midst of Samara and Galilee.
>
> 12 Then as He entered a certain village, there met Him ten men who were lepers, who stood afar off.
>
> 13 And they lifted up their voices and said, "Jesus, Master, have mercy on us!"

14 So when He saw them, He said to them, "Go, show yourselves to the priests." And so it was that as they went, they were cleansed.

15 And one of them, when he saw that he was healed, returned, and WITH A LOUD VOICE GLORIFIED GOD. (Emphasis added)

16 and fell down on his face at His feet, giving Him thanks. And he was a Samaritan.

17 So Jesus answered and said, "Were there not ten cleansed? But where are the nine?

18 "Were there not any found who returned TO GIVE GLORY TO GOD except this foreigner?" (Emphasis added)

Now at first, they were not giving glory to God. They were saying, "Jesus, have mercy on us! We are lepers!" They were not giving God the glory at first, but then one of them (after he was healed) was appreciative of his healing and went back and with a loud voice glorified God. He was not reserved about it either; he glorified God with a loud voice!

Acts 3:1-8

1 Now Peter and John went up together to the temple at the hour of prayer, the ninth hour.

2 And a certain man lame from his mother's womb was carried, whom they laid daily at the gate of the temple which is called Beautiful, to ask alms from those who entered the temple;

3 who, seeing Peter and John about to go into the temple, asked for alms.

4 And fixing his eyes on him, with John, Peter said, "Look at us."

5 So he gave them his attention, expecting to receive something from them.

> 6 Then Peter said, "Silver and gold I do not have, but what I do have I give you: In the name of Jesus Christ of Nazareth, rise up and walk."
> 7 And he took him by the right hand and lifted him up, and immediately his feet and ankle bones received strength.
> 8 So he, leaping up, stood and walked and entered the temple with them—walking, leaping, and PRAISING GOD. (Emphasis added)

We did not see the lame man praising God when he begged, "Alms for the poor, alms for the poor. Does anybody have money for a poor man?" No, he was not giving God any praise then. He gave God praise when he received his healing. As he was walking and leaping, he began to praise and worship God.

> Acts 4:21
> 21 So when they had further threatened them, they let them go, finding no way of punishing them, because of the people, since THEY ALL GLORIFIED GOD for what had been done. (Emphasis added)

This man was forty years old. He was laid daily at the gate of the temple that was called Beautiful. He received his healing, and he gave God the praise and the glory. God is glorified when people are healed, not when they are sick. The healing of the lame man also resulted in others giving glory to God for his deliverance.

"He sent His word and healed them." (Psalm 107:20). God does not want His people sick. To say that our Father God would put sickness on us is saying, without realizing it, that we are better parents than God. And the Bible says, "If you then, being evil, know how to give good gifts to your children, how much more will your Father...give good things to those who ask Him!" (Matthew 7:11).

God Is Not Guilty of Child Abuse

We would not punish or train our children by sitting them on a hot stove. They call that child abuse. And that is pretty sad if somebody does that. But do you know what is really sad? There are Christians who accuse God the Father of child abuse. When they say, "God put this on me," they are accusing God of child abuse. God does not do that with His kids any more than we would. We are no better parents than God. He is the perfect example of a Fatherly figure. He would not do anything to hurt us.

"For whom the Lord loves He chastens." (Hebrews 12:6). The word *chasten* in the Greek means "to child train". You do not train your child by causing harm to come on them. The way that God chastens us is by His Word, not by sickness or disease. God wants His people well. That is how God gets the glory.

> Luke 18:35-43
> 35 Then it happened, as He was coming near Jericho, that a certain blind man sat by the road begging.
> 36 And hearing a multitude passing by, he asked what it meant.
> 37 So they told him that Jesus of Nazareth was passing by.
> 38 And he cried out, saying, "Jesus, Son of David, have mercy on me!"
> 39 Then those who went before warned him that he should be quiet; but he cried out all the more, "Son of David, have mercy on me!"
> 40 So Jesus stood still and commanded him to be brought to Him. And when he had come near, He asked him,
> 41 saying, "What do you want Me to do for you?" He said, "Lord, that I may receive my sight."
> 42 Then Jesus said to him, "Receive your sight; your faith has made you well."

43 And immediately he received his sight, and followed Him, GLORIFYING GOD. And all the people, when they saw it, GAVE PRAISE TO GOD. (Emphasis added)

People get healed by being determined like this man was. If people really want to be healed, they have to want it bad enough.

Many people do not have faith for healing because they have never heard that God wants them well. That is the reason why some people need to be taught before they can receive their healing. Give the Word to them before laying hands on them so that faith for their healing can come. Many do not receive their healing because of a lack of faith. You will hear them say, "I am just hoping and praying. "They are not going to get anything like that. Hope is good, but you have got to do more than hope. You must be in faith.

The man in Luke, Chapter 18, had persistent faith. This man cried after Jesus, "Jesus, Son of David, have mercy on me!" People tried to shut him up, but he just got louder. This man was bold. He was determined. Verses 40 and 41 say, "So Jesus stood still and commanded him to be brought to Him. And when he had come near, He asked him, saying, 'What do you want Me to do for you?' "

Why did Jesus ask that question? Jesus knew what this man wanted. Jesus had sense enough to know that this man wanted to see. Actually, what He was doing was looking for a response of faith from this man. He came to Jesus as blind as a bat! It was obvious he wanted to be healed of his blindness; he wanted to see and Jesus knew that.

Faith Is Released by Words Through Your Mouth

Jesus said to him, "'What do you want Me to do for you?' He said, 'Lord, that I may receive my sight.'" This confession was the man's faith in action. Faith is released by words through your mouth. Then Jesus said to him, "'Receive your sight; your faith has made you well.' And immediately he received his sight, and followed Him, GLORIFYING GOD." (Emphasis added)

He was not glorifying God when he cried out, "Jesus, Son of David, have mercy on me!" We did not see him glorifying God when he was blind. But once he received his sight, he glorified God! Verse 43 says, "And immediately he received his sight, and followed Him, glorifying God. And all the people, when they saw it, gave praise to God."

There was not any shouting, any praising, or any glorifying of God going on while the man was blind. But when the people saw he was healed, they glorified God. Immediately, when the man was healed, he glorified God. God gets the glory when people are made whole. Can you see this pattern being weaved throughout the Word of God?

> 1 Corinthians 12:27
> 27 Now you are the body of Christ, and members individually.

> Ephesians1: 22-23
> 22 And He put all things under His feet, and gave Him to be head over all things to the church,
> 23 which is His body, the fullness of Him who fills all in all.

The Church is the body of Christ. Jesus is the head and we are the body.

> 1 Corinthians 6:19-20
> 19 Or do you not know that your body is the temple of the Holy Spirit who is in you, whom you have from God, and you are not your own?
> 20 For you were bought at a price; therefore glorify God in your body and in your spirit, which are God's.

Notice verse 19 says, "Your body is the temple of the Holy Spirit who is in you, whom you have from God, and you are not your own?" Your body does not even belong to you. I know that we will get a new, glorified body in heaven, but we need to do something about our bodies down here on the earth. Your body is not even yours.

"For you were bought at a price; therefore glorify God in your body and in your spirit, which are God's" (1 Corinthians 6:20). The Bible says to glorify God in your body and your spirit. Give Him glory in your body. One way you glorify God in your body is to keep your body from sin and bring it into subjection to God's will.

Glorifying God in your body also means to keep sickness and disease away from your body. That is your responsibility. God is not glorified when your body is sick. We have seen in the Word of God that He gets the glory when people are well. God gets the glory when you are well.

When Jesus walked on this earth, He was the body of Christ on the earth. He was the only body of Christ on the earth at that time. Jesus never permitted sickness and disease in His body.

People always want to bring up Paul. "Well, Paul was a sick man all of his life." When did Paul die for you? When was Paul raised from the dead? When was Paul seated at the right hand of the Father for you? Now as we have stated earlier, Paul was not sick all of his life, as some people would like to believe. But what if he was? Even if he was sick all of his life, he is not my example.

Well, what about Job? Job was not sick all his life, either. But even if he was, when did Job die for you? When was Job raised from the dead? When was Job seated at the right hand of the Father? Job is not your example either.

When have you ever heard of Jesus being sick? Read Matthew, Mark, Luke, and John. When was Jesus ever sick? Not only did He not permit sickness in His body, But He also did not permit sickness and disease around Him either. Acts 10:38 says, "Who [Jesus] went about doing good and healing all who were oppressed by the devil, for God was with Him."

The Bible says Jesus healed the multitude's sick. I do not even remember His disciples being sick. Nobody could hang around Jesus too long without being healed. Jesus glorified God in His body. Jesus died for us. Jesus was raised from the dead. And Jesus is seated at the right hand of the Father.

Jesus is the head of the Church, and we are the body of Christ. If He did not want His body to be sick when He walked the earth, why would He want His body sick now? Jesus did not allow sickness in His body when He walked the earth. He did not allow His body to be sick. God does not want sickness in His body today. We are the body of Christ. The Bible says, "For you were bought at a price; therefore glorify God in your body" (1 Corinthians 6:20).

You can do more for God when you are well than you can when you are in a hospital. "Well, the Lord's got a purpose for me being in the hospital." No, He does not! You can do more for God when you are walking in divine health.

Some say, "Well, look at what Paul did, and he was sick all of his life." As we have already said, Paul was not sick all of his life. They tried to stone him, and they left him for dead. Did they take him to the hospital? NO! He got up and started preaching the next day in another city. That does not sound like a sick man!

They stoned the man. They stoned him and left him for dead. He got up and went on preaching. He did not even go to the hospital as an outpatient. He started preaching the very next day.

8.
Redeemed from the Curse of Sickness

Christ has redeemed us from the curse of the law, having become a curse for us (for it is written, "Cursed is everyone who hangs on a tree"), that the blessing of Abraham might come upon the Gentiles in Christ Jesus, that we might receive the promise of the Spirit through faith.
—Galatians 3:13,14

These verses tell us that Christ has redeemed us from the curse of the Law. The Law refers to the first five books of the Bible also known as the Pentateuch. Redeem means to buy back. We were in bondage to Satan, and Christ came to redeem us from Satan and the curse of God's violated law.

To be redeemed from the curse means that we are no longer where the curse is. For example, if you are living in Orlando, but you were born in Atlanta, it is obvious that where you are now (Orlando) is not where you are from. Since we are redeemed from the curse, we are no longer where the curse is (we are redeemed from there).

We also need to know what we have been redeemed to. Verse 14 says, "That the blessings of Abraham might come upon the Gentiles in Christ Jesus, that we might receive the promise of the Spirit through faith". We have been redeemed to the blessings.

The curse of the Law is threefold: Poverty, sickness, and spiritual death. Deuteronomy, Chapter 28, lists the blessings and the curses of the law. Since we are on the subject of divine healing, I want to focus on the curse of sickness. Sickness is not a blessing; it is a curse. Let us go to the Bible and look at this curse.

Deuteronomy 28:15

15 "But it shall come to pass, if you do not obey the voice of the LORD your God, to observe carefully all His commandments and His statutes which I command you today, that all these curses will come upon you and overtake you"

Deuteronomy 28:18

18 "Cursed shall be the fruit of your body and the produce of your land, the increase of your cattle and the offspring of your flocks."

Deuteronomy 28:21, 22

21 "The LORD will make the plague cling to you until He has consumed you from the land which you are going to possess.
22 "The LORD will strike you with consumption, with fever, with inflammation, with severe burning fever, with the sword, with scorching, and with mildew; they shall pursue you until you perish."

Deuteronomy 28:27-29

27 "The LORD will strike you with the boils of Egypt, with tumors, with the scab, and with the itch, from which you cannot be healed.
28 "The LORD will strike you with madness and blindness and confusion of heart.
29 "And you shall grope at noonday, as a blind man gropes in darkness; you shall not prosper in your ways; you shall be only oppressed and plundered continually, and no one shall save you."

Deuteronomy 28:35

35 "The LORD will strike you in the knees and on the legs with severe boils which cannot be healed, and from the sole of your foot to the top of your head."

Deuteronomy 28:58-61

58 "If you do not carefully observe all the words of this law that are written in this book, that you may fear this glorious and awesome name, THE LORD YOUR GOD, (Emphasis added)

59 "then the LORD will bring upon you and your descendants extraordinary plagues—great and prolonged plagues— and serious and prolonged sicknesses.

60 "Moreover He will bring back on you all the diseases of Egypt, of which you were afraid, and they shall cling to you.

61 "Also every sickness and every plague, which is not written in this Book of the Law, will the LORD bring upon you until you are destroyed."

Keep in mind what we have said earlier in the book about causative and permissive verbs. In reading these verses, it appears as though God is causing the sickness. But in the original Hebrew, the verbs are in the permissive sense rather than in the causative sense. So actually, it is God allowing or permitting the diseases to come upon the children of Israel if they did not keep His commandments.

Every sickness and disease known to mankind is covered here under the curse of the Law. The diseases that are not specifically mentioned by name are covered by verse 61. It says, "Also every sickness and every plague, which is not written in this Book of the Law."

This means we have been redeemed from every sickness and disease that exists!

Christ has redeemed us from the curse of the law, and sickness is a part of the curse that we have been redeemed from. We are free from sickness and disease!

But wait! What about what it says in Deuteronomy 28:1 and 2? Let us go there.

> Deuteronomy 28:1–2
> 1 "Now it shall come to pass, if you diligently obey the voice of the Lord your God, to observe carefully all His commandments which I command you today, that the Lord your God will set you high above all nations of the earth.
> 2 And all these blessings shall come upon you and overtake you, because you obey the voice of the Lord your God:

Doesn't this say that we have to keep all the commandments to qualify for all the blessings that are listed in Deuteronomy 28?

That was true under the law. Under the law, if you obeyed all the commandments, you would be blessed. If you did not obey, you would be cursed.

Here is the good news. But we are not under the law. We are under grace. And in this New Covenant of grace, we only get the blessings.

Why do we only get the blessings? It is because of Jesus. He was our substitute. He did what we could not do - He kept the law perfectly. And He went to the cross to take away all of our sins (past, present, and future). He became sin for us, so we could become the righteousness of God, in Him. He took away all of the curses, so we could receive all of the blessings.

When we receive what Jesus did for us on the cross, none of the curses can fall on us, and we have a right to all of the blessings.

God Already Qualified You for Healing, so Do Not Try to Earn It

> Colossians 1:12–14
> 12 giving thanks to the Father who has qualified us to be partakers of the inheritance of the saints in the light.
> 13 He has delivered us from the power of darkness and conveyed us into the kingdom of the Son of His love,
> 14 in whom we have redemption through His blood, the forgiveness of sins.

Our inheritance includes healing. We do not have to qualify to receive our healing because God has already qualified us to partake of healing through the finished work of Jesus on the cross. We have redemption through His blood.

Therefore, you are not healed because of your good behavior or self-effort, you are healed because of God's grace or unmerited favor. You do not earn your healing. Jesus earned it for you.

9.
Discerning the Lord's Body

For I received from the Lord that which I also delivered to you: that the Lord Jesus on the same night in which He was betrayed took bread; and when He had given thanks, He broke it and said, "Take, eat; this is My body which is broken for you; do this in remembrance of Me." In the same manner He also took the cup after supper, saying, "This cup is the new covenant in My blood. This do, as often as you drink it, in remembrance of Me." For as often as you eat this bread and drink this cup, you proclaim the Lord's death till He comes. Therefore whoever eats this bread or drinks this cup of the Lord in an UNWORTHY MANNER will be guilty of the body and blood of the Lord. (Emphasis added) But let a man examine himself, and so let him eat of the bread and drink of the cup. For he who eats and drinks in an unworthy manner eats and drinks judgment to himself, not discerning the Lord's body. FOR THIS REASON MANY ARE WEAK AND SICK AMONG YOU, AND MANY SLEEP. (Emphasis added) For if we would judge ourselves, we would not be judged. But when we are judged, we are chastened by the Lord, that we may not be condemned with the world.
—1 Corinthians 11:23-32

Discern means "to see and understand." The last part of verse 29 can be restated as, "Not understanding the Lord's body." Now in verse 30 it says, "For this reason..." For what reason? Not understanding the Lord's body is the reason. Continuing with this verse, it says, "...many are weak and sick among you, and many sleep [die]."

"By whose [Jesus] stripes you were healed" (1 Peter 2:24). We need to understand that the Lord's body was broken for our sicknesses and our diseases. Many are sick, weak, and die in the Church because they do not understand that Jesus took their sicknesses.

Look at verse 23. Paul received the truth concerning the Lord's Supper by revelation from the Lord. Paul was not there when the Lord's Supper was instituted. But Paul described what actually happened as if he were there.

The fact that the Lord shared it with Paul lets us know that the Lord's Supper is very important. It is not something that should be taken lightly nor casually. It is an ordinance of the Church. Verse 27 says that we should not eat (the bread) or drink (the cup) in an unworthy manner. You do that by not appropriating the benefits for which it stands. The Lord's Supper stands for something. It represents something.

Verse 30 contains an astounding truth. Many Christians are actually physically weak, sick in body, and even die simply because they do not understand the Lord's body. Many people take communion, and they do not understand what the Lord's Supper represents. We need to know what we are doing when we partake of the Lord's Supper. We need to rightly discern, see, and understand the Lord's body.

We need to understand that the body of Christ was broken for our sicknesses and diseases, and we have a right to live in divine health. Healing is one of the benefits of Calvary.

> Psalm 103:1-3
> 1 Bless the LORD, O my soul;
> And all that is within me, bless His holy name!
> 2 Bless the LORD, O my soul,
> And forget not all His benefits:
> 3 Who forgives all your iniquities,
> Who heals all your diseases,

If Jesus healed all of our diseases, that means that legally we do not have any diseases. He took them. Because people do not understand that, many are physically weak, many are sick in their body, and many die before they are supposed to.

By His stripes, you *were* healed (1Peter 2:24). And because you *were* healed, you are not trying to get healed. You *are* already healed because you were healed a long time ago! So, see yourself healed now.

10.
Dealing with Sickness and Tragedy in the Church

No one engaged in warfare entangles himself with the affairs of this life, that he may please him who enlisted him as a SOLDIER. (Emphasis added)
—2 Timothy 2:3,4

You Therefore Must Endure Hardship as a Good Soldier of Jesus Christ

We need to realize that we as Christians are in warfare. In any warfare, there are causalities. As I said before, we should aim for God's best as our target, but we also need to realize that everyone is not going to attain God's best. We do not always know why a believer in Christ is sick or dies.

We are in warfare, and there will be Christians who will suffer loss, sickness, and tragedy. That is not God's will; it is not His best, but it will happen. We need to know how to effectively minister to people who suffer loss. The Word of God instructs us to walk in love. In ministering to people, we should not be rough, cold, and callous to those who suffer sickness or tragedy. We should minister to them in love. We should not condemn them but rather exhort, edify, and comfort them.

The following are instructions to help you in ministering to those who are suffering with sickness.

1. Review Basic Healing Scriptures with Them, Such as Isaiah 53:5, Matthew 8:17, 1 Peter 2:24, and Psalm 103:1-3

2. Assure Them That God Did Not Cause the Sickness

> John 10:10
> 10 "The thief does not come except to steal, and to kill, and to destroy. I have come that they may have life, and that they may have it more abundantly."

Speaking the Truth in Love

> Ephesians 4:15
> 15 but, speaking the truth in love, may grow up in all things into Him who is the head—Christ—

The Word exhorts us here to speak the truth in love. We must not lie to those who are suffering with sickness and disease. Telling them things like, "God put this on them to teach them something," or "God has a purpose in this sickness." This is not true! God does not put sickness on people to teach them something. Although many people say that, they do not really believe it because they go to the doctor to get help. If you really believe God was teaching you a lesson, would you miss your lesson by going to the doctor to get well?

It is also untrue that God has a purpose in you being sick. Sickness is of the devil, and the devil is the one who has a purpose in putting sickness on you. He wants to steal, kill, and destroy. John 10:10 tells us that, "The thief does not come except to steal, and to kill, and to destroy." Satan is the thief, and he is the source of the sickness and the disease, not God.

You comfort the sick by being there for them and ministering to them, not by lying to them. Speaking the truth is not condemning if it is done in love.

Suppose you were to go to a doctor with symptoms of weakness and fatigue. If the doctor tells you that you do not have enough vitamins in your diet, you do not get mad at the doctor and accuse him of putting condemnation on you, do you? No, you simply do what he says to eliminate the problem. The doctor is not trying to put you in condemnation; he is trying to help you.

Luke 8:22-25

22 Now it happened, on a certain day, that He got into a boat with His disciples. And He said to them, "Let us cross over to the other side of the lake." And they launched out.

23 But as they sailed He fell asleep. And a windstorm came down on the lake, and they were filling with water, and were in jeopardy.

24 And they came to Him and awoke Him, saying, "Master, Master, we are perishing!" Then He arose and rebuked the wind and the raging of the water. And they ceased, and there was a calm.

25 But He said to them, "Where is your faith?" And they were afraid, and marveled, saying to one another, "Who can this be? For He commands even the winds and water, and they obey Him!"

Jesus says in verse 25, "Where is your faith?" When He said that, He was not trying to put them in condemnation; He was simply trying to help them. Jesus said in John 8:32, "And you shall know the truth, and the truth shall make you free." Knowing the truth does not put you in bondage; it makes you free! Jesus pointed out their lack of faith and that let them know, specifically, why they could not rebuke the wind and water.

The disciples received the chastening of the Lord. It is a sign of humility to receive correction. On the other hand, pride causes some people to think that they could not possibly be at fault.

Matthew 17:14-21

14 And when they had come to the multitude, a man came to Him, kneeling down to Him and saying,

15 "Lord, have mercy on my son, for he is an epileptic and suffers severely; for he often falls into the fire and often into the water.

16 "So I brought him to Your disciples, but they could not cure him."

17 Then Jesus answered and said, "O faithless and perverse generation, how long shall I be with you? How long shall I bear with you? Bring him here to Me."

18 And Jesus rebuked the demon, and it came out of him; and the child was cured from that very hour.

19 Then the disciples came to Jesus privately and said, "Why could we not cast it out?"

20 So Jesus said to them, "Because of your unbelief; for assuredly, I say to you, if you have faith as a mustard seed, you will say to this mountain, 'Move from here to there,' and it will move; and nothing will be impossible for you.

21 "However, this kind does not go out except by prayer and fasting."

Here is another example of failure resulting from a lack of faith. A man said he brought his son to Jesus' disciples, and they could not cast the demon out. Actually, that was not a statement of truth. It was not a matter of the disciples not being able to cast the demon out, because Jesus gave them the authority to cast out demons and to heal the sick.

The truth is, they could have cast him out, but they did not because they did not use the authority God gave them. They failed to get the job done. After Jesus cast the demon out of the child, the disciples asked Jesus why they could not do the same. Jesus did not hesitate or beat around the bush. He went straight to the point and told them the reason was due to their unbelief.

Jesus operated in the principle that knowing the truth will make you free. Jesus did not tell them this to put them in bondage or condemnation but to set them free and to help them so that the next time they face a demon, they would be successful.

Hebrews 12:5-9

5 And you have forgotten the exhortation which speaks to you as to sons: "My son, do not despise the chastening of the LORD, Nor be discouraged when you are rebuked by Him;
6 For whom the LORD loves He chastens, And scourges every son whom He receives."
7 If you endure chastening, God deals with you as with sons; for what son is there whom a father does not chasten?
8 But if you are without chastening, of which all have become partakers, then you are illegitimate and not sons.
9 Furthermore, we have had human fathers who corrected us, and we paid them respect. Shall we not much more readily be in subjection to the Father of spirits and live?

Hebrews 12:6 is a quote from Proverbs.

Proverbs 3:12
12 For whom the LORD loves He corrects, Just as a father the son in whom he delights.

Hebrews 12:11
11 Now no chastening seems to be joyful for the present, but painful; nevertheless, afterward it yields the peaceable fruit of righteousness to those who have been trained by it.

This shows us that to chasten means to correct. We all need correction, but God does not correct us by putting sickness and disease on us.

> Matthew 7:11
> 11 If you then, being evil, know how to give good gifts to your children, how much more will your Father who is in heaven give good things to those who ask Him!

If we as humans would not correct our children by putting their hand on a hot stove, then why do we think God would chasten us by putting sickness on us? We are not better parents than God.

The way God chastens us is through His Word. The reason why many Christians do not grow spiritually is that they do not submit to the correction of the Word of God. However, when sickness or tragedy occurs, many Christians automatically say, "It must be God's will." But that statement reflects ignorance of God's Word.

To blame everything on God is to take all responsibility away from ourselves. When Christians have the attitude that they could not possibly do anything wrong, that is not humility but pride.

Hebrews 12:11 says, "Now no chastening seems to be joyful for the present, but painful." The truth may hurt you at first. But if you receive the chastening, "nevertheless, afterward it yields the peaceable fruit of righteousness to those who have been trained by it." If I need to develop more faith, I want to know about it so I can work on developing my faith for the next challenge I face.

3. Do Not Concern Yourself with Why the Sickness or Tragedy Happened to You

> Deuteronomy 29:29
> 29 "The secret things belong to the LORD our God, but those things which are revealed belong to us and to our children forever, that we may do all the words of this law."

This verse tells us, "The secret things belong to the LORD our God, but those things which are revealed belong to us." You can apply this to a sickness or a tragedy. Sometimes when a person is sick or is in a tragedy, it is a secret thing that belongs to the Lord. That simply means there are times when things happen which we do not understand, and it is not for us to know.

This verse says that those things, which are revealed, belong to us. If God reveals to you the reason why something happens, then receive it. If something has not been revealed to you, then it is a secret thing that belongs to God. You should not concern yourself with it. In other words, if the reason why has not been revealed to you, it does not belong to you. It belongs to God, so leave it alone.

Once you are in a difficult situation, the emphasis should be placed on how to get out of it, not how you got into it. In many cases, people are so busy concerning themselves with why this is happening to them that they do not do what is necessary to get the victory in the situation. If God does not specifically deal with you as to the cause of the sickness or circumstance that you are in, do what you know to do to get yourself out of the circumstance.

4. Deal with the Solution

Find scriptures that address the individual's sickness or problem. Find scriptures that specifically deal with the situation the individual is facing.

Now I want to give you a practical suggestion on how to minister to someone who has suffered a tragedy or the loss of a loved one. The key is to look to the Holy Spirit for wisdom on what to say and how to say it. Be sure that you comfort them and not condemn them or make any offensive remarks to them.

It is not comforting to hear statements like: "You should have had more faith", or "If you would have had more faith, this tragedy would not have happened." Those remarks are unwise and inappropriate when someone has just suffered a tragedy or loss.

The faith message has suffered a black eye due to a few people who make ignorant statements such as these. That is a good way to turn people off. We need to remember that people are at different stages of faith and their spiritual development. We need to learn how to meet people where they are at their level of faith.

11.

How to Minister to the Sick Through the Laying on of Hands

And these signs will follow those who believe: In My name they will cast out demons; they will speak with new tongues; they will take up serpents; and if they drink anything deadly, it will by no means hurt them; THEY WILL LAY HANDS ON THE SICK, AND THEY WILL RECOVER. So then, after the Lord had spoken to them, He was received up into heaven, and sat down at the right hand of God. And they went out and preached everywhere, the Lord working with them and confirming the word through the accompanying signs. Amen.
—Mark 16:17-20 (Emphasis added)

Laying on of hands is one way, not the only way, to minister healing to the sick. The following are some tips on how to minister to the sick through the laying on of hands.

1. Set the Environment for Healing

The right atmosphere is important when ministering healing to someone. An environment charged with unbelief can greatly hinder the healing process. On the other hand, an environment of faith can make it easy for a person to receive their healing.

Sometimes you have to put people out of the room. This action takes boldness but sometimes is necessary when unbelief is in the air. It will keep you from having to cut through unbelief. That does not mean you have to be gruff or make a big scene. You can kindly ask them to step out of the room for a few moments while you spend some time alone with the individual. There is really no point in aggravating anyone.

Acts 9:39, 40

39 Then Peter arose and went with them. When he had come, they brought him to the upper room. And all the widows stood by him weeping, showing the tunics and garments which Dorcas had made while she was with them.

40 But Peter PUT THEM ALL OUT, and knelt down and prayed. And turning to the body he said, "Tabitha, arise." And she opened her eyes, and when she saw Peter she sat up. (Emphasis added)

Here was a situation where Peter needed to raise the dead. When he arrived, he faced a scene where people were crying over things that reminded them of the deceased.

But Peter, having been with Jesus on a similar occasion, remembered what Jesus did when He faced the same type of circumstances—He put everybody out. And the reason He did that was because the mourners would not have contributed to an environment of faith. He had the spiritual sensitivity to recognize that they would only be a hindrance to Him raising the dead.

It is easy to overlook the point that Peter cleared the room to focus on raising Dorcas from the dead. The raising of the dead was supernatural and spectacular; it was the end result. But, interestingly, the Holy Spirit saw fit to preface this miracle by showing us how Peter created the right atmosphere to produce this result.

I do not believe the Holy Spirit would have put this point in here if it were not significant. I believe that removing everyone from the room was necessary in order to raise Dorcas from the dead. Something else was significant here. Notice that before Peter spoke to the body, he prayed. I believe that he prayed in tongues to build himself up.

1 Corinthians 14:4
4 He who speaks in a tongue edifies himself [or builds himself up], but he who prophesies edifies the church.

Now you cannot prove from the Bible that tongues was the type of praying that he did, but you cannot disprove it either.

1 Corinthians 12:9
9 to another FAITH by the same Spirit, to another gifts of healings by the same Spirit, (Emphasis added)

1 Corinthians 12:9 (AMP)
9 To another [wonder-working] faith by the same [Holy] Spirit, to another the extraordinary powers of healing by the one Spirit;

The faith spoken of here is not ordinary faith that every believer has. This is a manifestation of special faith. When Peter spoke to the dead body, that was special faith in operation. When he spoke the word of faith to the body in the power of the Spirit, the body responded to the spoken Word, and Dorcas was raised from the dead.

Luke 8:49-56
49 While He was still speaking, someone came from the ruler of the synagogue's house, saying to him, "Your daughter is dead. Do not trouble the Teacher."
50 But when Jesus heard it, He answered him, saying, "Do not be afraid; only believe, and she will be made well."
51 When He came into the house, He permitted no one to go in except Peter, James, and John, and the father and mother of the girl.

> 52 Now all wept and mourned for her; but He said, "Do not weep; she is not dead, but sleeping."
> 53 And they ridiculed Him, knowing that she was dead.
> 54 But He PUT THEM ALL OUTSIDE, took her by the hand and called, saying, "Little girl, arise." (Emphasis added)
> 55 Then her spirit returned, and she arose immediately. And He commanded that she be given something to eat.
> 56 And her parents were astonished, but He charged them to tell no one what had happened.

Now here was a situation where Jesus raised the dead. Notice that Jesus did not just charge into the house and command the dead to rise. He first created an atmosphere that was conducive to raising the dead.

Verse 51 says, "He permitted no one to go in except Peter, James, and John [His inner circle], and the father and mother of the girl." He did not even allow all of the disciples to go into the house. He was very selective as to whom He wanted to go in with Him because He wanted to create the proper environment for raising the dead.

Once He entered the house, there were people crying and mourning. When Jesus said to them "She is not dead, but sleeping," they ridiculed Him (Luke 8:52). The NIV said they laughed at him, knowing that she was dead. But Jesus did not argue with the people in the house or try to persuade them. He took charge of the situation and put all the people out. When He did, He cleared the air of unbelief and created the proper environment for raising the dead.

2. Show the Candidate for Healing That It Is God's Will for Them to Be Well

Explain from the Word how healing belongs to them and was purchased for them at Calvary. Some basic scriptures are Isaiah 53:5,

Matthew 8:17, 1 Peter 2:24, and Psalm 103:1-3. For detailed information on these scriptures, refer to chapter 3 of this book.

3. Explain That the Laying on of Hands Is One of the Doctrines of the Church

> Hebrews 6:1, 2
> 1 Therefore, leaving the discussion of the elementary principles of Christ, let us go on to perfection, not laying again the foundation of repentance from dead works and of faith toward God,
> 2 of the doctrine of baptisms, of LAYING ON OF HANDS, of resurrection of the dead, and of eternal judgment. (Emphasis added)

Jesus said that believers will lay hands on the sick.

> Mark 16:17,18
> 17 "And these signs will follow THOSE WHO BELIEVE: In My name they will cast out demons; they will speak with new tongues; (Emphasis added)
> 18 "they will take up serpents; and if they drink anything deadly, it will by no means hurt them; they will lay hands on the sick, and they will recover."

Some people say, "I do not believe in laying hands on the sick." Well, by saying that you disqualify yourself from this working for you because Jesus said the signs shall only follow those who believe. So if you do not believe, it will not work for you.

One of the signs mentioned in verse 18 is that they will lay hands on the sick, and they will recover. The word *recovery* implies a process —going from a point of being sick to a point of being well.

We need to explain to the candidate that if they do not receive an instant manifestation of healing, it does not mean that they are not healed. A person need not be discouraged if they are not instantly healed when hands are laid on them for healing. Sometimes the reason they are discouraged is that they are not taught how to receive their healing by faith.

Another important thing to know about laying on of hands is that it is a transmission of power. When hands are laid on a person in Jesus' Name, power flows from the person who is ministering to the person who is sick.

4. Explain the Prayer of Faith

> Mark 11:24
> 24 "Therefore I say to you, whatever things you ask WHEN YOU PRAY, believe that you receive them, and you will have them. (Emphasis added)

You must believe that you receive healing when you pray. And when you do that, it is yours by faith (it is a faith fact) in the realm of the Spirit.

If you believe you receive when you pray (that is the faith part), you shall receive the manifestation.

Let us look at the words believe that you receive. Notice it does not say, feel like you receive. It says, "BELIEVE THAT YOU RECEIVE". You do not have to have a feeling, and you should not expect a feeling when you pray. God answering your prayer has nothing to do with how you feel at the time of prayer. You receive by faith, not by feeling.

Some people are waiting to see something before they believe it, and that is the MAN KIND OF FAITH. The man kind of faith says SEEING IS BELIEVING. But notice that Mark 11:24 tells us we are to believe that we receive, and we will have them. There is no seeing or sight involved in believing that you receive. Believe that you receive is your faith in operation.

Believe that you receive is PRESENT TENSE. You will have is FUTURE TENSE. You will have is the manifestation or the end result. So you must believe before you can see the manifestation. *You will have* is based on *believing that you receive*. Believing that you receive is the faith fact. You will have is the physical or tangible fact.

The phrase *seeing is believing* is contrary to the Word of God. Not only that, it is an incorrect statement. Seeing is not believing—seeing is knowing. If you see something, you do not have to believe it because you know it. You only have to believe something when you do not see it. The God kind of faith says BELIEVING WILL CAUSE SEEING. When you have to believe something, that tells you, you do not have it or see it yet.

There is nothing to feel or see at the time of prayer. You must believe that you receive when you pray. And you must not have the manifestation when you pray. You would not need to believe for something you already have in manifestation. Mark 11:24 says, "Believe that you receive them, and you SHALL HAVE them." *Shall have* has to do with the manifestation. So believe that you receive healing, and you shall have healing!

Now some people bring up a question concerning God's sovereignty. What about the sovereignty of God? Is God sovereign? Certainly, He is. When people hear teaching that you can receive your healing by asking and believing God and expecting Him to heal you, some people just cannot comprehend that. They think that you cannot expect God to heal you anytime you get ready because they believe it takes away the sovereignty of God.

Believing that God will heal you when you receive your healing by faith does not take away the sovereignty of God? God's Word is sovereign. And God will not violate or contradict His Word. God limits Himself by His Word. He binds Himself by His Word. God cannot lie. God is a covenant-keeping God. God has obligated Himself, He has bound Himself, and He has restricted Himself to His Word. He will only operate within the confines of His Word. And that is God's sovereignty.

You see, God's Word, as indicated in Mark 11:24, is sovereign. "Therefore I say to you, whatever things you ask when you pray, believe that you receive them, and you will have them." That is sovereign. Now, whose Word is this? We have to be convinced, first of all, that this is God's Word that we are reading.

Matthew 8:17 says, "He Himself took our infirmities and bore our sicknesses." This was a sovereign act of God's will. God sovereignly bore our sicknesses through Jesus at Calvary. "By whose stripes you were healed" (1 Peter 2:24). We do not have to convince God to heal us. He already has. We need to realize that the time of healing has already taken place. What we are doing is just receiving the healing that already belongs to us.

5. Get Feedback to Make Sure They Understand Their Responsibility

I have found that in ministering to the sick, it is important to find out if that person understands what the Word says and understands what their responsibility is. Even though hands are laid on them and the prayer of faith has been prayed over them, they have a responsibility to exercise faith for themselves in order to see the results.

The candidate needs to understand how to make a confession of faith. Later in this book, I will give an example of how to make faith confessions based on God's Word.

Instruct them to thank God for their healing until the manifestation comes.

> Hebrews 13:15
> 15 Therefore by Him let us continually offer the sacrifice of praise to God, that is, the fruit of our lips, giving thanks to His name.

After you believe you receive when you pray, it is important to thank God for your healing. Give Him praise and glorify His Name.

In ministering to the sick through the laying on of hands, many people seem to think that 'all' you have to do is get someone to pray for you and then 'wait and see' if something happens. You must know what to do after hands are laid on you and the prayer of faith has been prayed for you.

It Is After Prayer When Most Healing Is Lost

Many people lose their healing after they have been prayed for. Let us look at an example of what to do after hands are laid on you for healing.

Let us say someone lays hands on you on October 24th and, according to Mark 11:24, you believe you receive at that moment. You now have your healing by faith, no matter what it looks like or how you feel. And you have based your healing on scriptures: "He Himself took your infirmities and bore your sicknesses" (Matthew 8:17); and "By whose stripes, you were healed" (1 Peter 2:24). You do not have to wait and see if it is God's will for you to be healed because you were (past tense) healed at Calvary. Now on October 25th, in your prayer time, you do not ask for your healing because you received your healing on October 24th. So begin to thank and praise God for your healing!

6. Leave Faith-Filled Materials (Books and Cds) on the Subject of Grace, Faith, and Healing

Word-based books and CDs help to give instruction and reinforce the scriptural truths on the subject of healing. Encourage the candidate to study the material thoroughly. Here are some things they can do to make the information a part of them:

- Look up the scriptures presented in their own Bible (Acts 17:11).
- Underline or highlight key points.
- Take notes on the material.
- Teach the material to someone else.
- Act on what they have received by looking for creative ways to apply the Word to their situation (James 1:22).

12.
How to Deal with an Attack of Sickness and Disease

No matter how strong you are in the Word of God, Satan will from time to time endeavor to steal your health by attacking you with sickness and disease. I want to share with you how to stand against an attack of sickness when it tries to come on your body.

> Joel 3:10
> 10 "Beat your plowshares into swords And your pruning hooks into spears; LET THE WEAK SAY, 'I AM STRONG.'" (Emphasis added)

This verse says, "Let the weak say, 'I am strong.'" Some people think that if you are weak, you should say you are weak, otherwise, you are telling a lie. But that is not true according to the Bible.

> Mark 11:23
> 23 For assuredly, I say to you, whoever says to this mountain, 'Be removed and be cast into the sea,' and does not doubt in his heart, but believes that those things he says will be done, he will have whatever he says.

Romans 4:17 says, "[God] calls those things which do not exist as though they did." Ephesians 5:1 says we are to be imitators of God as dear children. So, like our Father, we are to do the same thing He does and call those things that be not as though they were. Jesus says in Mark 11:23, "He will have whatever he says."

The Bible says, "Let the weak say, 'I am strong'" (Joel 3:10). So we can use that same principle in the area of healing, and we can say, "Let the sick say, 'I am healed.'" The sick should not say, "I am sick," if they want to be healed. To be healed, the sick must learn to say what they want, not what they have. Therefore, the sick should say, "I am healed," not because they look like it or because they feel like it but because of what the Word says.

The Word says, "He Himself took my infirmities and bore my sicknesses" (Matthew 8:17). It also says, "By whose stripes you were healed" (1 Peter 2:24). If I were healed then I am healed, and if I am healed then "I is" healed. And I believe that "I is" healed. I do not see myself as sick, so I do not call myself sick—I call myself healed. By doing that, you are not lying; you are just saying what God says about your body rather than saying how you feel.

2 Corinthians 5:7
7 For we walk by faith, not by sight.

Smith Wigglesworth made a classic statement years ago. He said, "I am not moved by what I see, I am not moved by how I feel, I am moved only by what I believe." We need to learn how to walk by the Word and not by our feelings. Feelings are irrelevant. To walk by faith is to walk by the Word.

Romans 10:8
8 But what does it say? "The word is near you, in your mouth and in your heart" (that is, the WORD OF FAITH which we preach): (Emphasis added)

This says that the Word of God is the word of faith, which we preach. The Word of God is a faith producing Word.

Romans 10:17
17 So then faith comes by hearing, and hearing by the word of God.

Faith comes by hearing and hearing by the Word of God. That is because the Word of God, when preached, produces faith in the hearts of the hearers.

Until you have the Word, you have no faith because faith comes by the Word. So whenever the Word of God is present, faith is present. Therefore, faith and the Word are synonymous terms. When you have faith, you have the Word; and when you have the Word, you have faith. Since faith and the Word are synonymous, we can rephrase 2 Corinthians 5:7 and read it this way, "For we walk by the Word, not by the senses." Walking by the Word of God is walking by faith.

Here is another way of putting it: when you are walking by faith, you are flying by the instruments. An airline pilot does not determine where he is going by looking out of his window. He is totally disoriented in terms of his sense of direction. He does not look to his senses to determine where he is or where he is headed.

The pilot is trained to fly by the instruments on his panel. It is irrelevant whether the pilot feels like he's going east or west. It does not make any difference what it looks like because he does not determine where he is by what it looks like. He determines where he is by what the instruments on the panel tell him.

So when you are walking by faith, you are walking by the Word. You are walking by what the Word of God tells you, not by how you feel or what you see. You are doing what the pilot does, flying by the instruments (of God's Word). So when symptoms come and your body feels sick, do not pay attention to your feelings. Only look at or pay attention to what the Word says about your body. The Word says, "By whose stripes, you were healed" (1 Peter 2:24).

> 2 Corinthians 4:18
> 18 while we do not look at the things which are seen,
> but at the things, which are not seen. For the things
> which are seen are temporary, but the things which
> are not seen are eternal.

This verse says, "We do not look at the things which are seen [or what it looks like], but at the things which are not seen." The things, which your senses tell, you are temporal, temporary, or subject to change. But the things, which are not seen, are eternal. In other words, the things in the unseen realm are not subject to change. The unseen realm is the realm where God is—the spirit realm.

Hebrews 11:1 says, "Now faith is the substance of things hoped for, the evidence of things not seen." Faith is then the evidence of things in the unseen realm—the spirit realm, where God is. And we found out that faith and the Word are synonymous terms. So we can substitute the Word for faith in Hebrews 11:1 and say, "The Word is the evidence of things not seen."

The Word tells me what is in God's realm—the realm of the spirit. When 1 Peter 2:24 says, "By whose stripes you were healed," this tells me that in the spirit realm, I am healed. And according to 2 Corinthians 4:18, that is what I should look at relative to healing, no matter how I feel or see. It is telling us to look at the healing that is in the unseen realm of God.

We should treat our feelings and the things, which are seen as temporal, temporary, or subject to change. Your symptoms will change as you walk by faith—as you walk by the Word. Focus on the things that belong to you. Look at the healing that belongs to you in the spirit realm.

You must develop such an unshakable confidence in God's Word that the Word of God becomes more real to you than the symptoms in your body. Even though symptoms may persist, you must be fully persuaded that the Word is much more powerful than the symptoms. As you continue to steadfastly look to the Word of God, the Word of God will remove the symptoms. It will push the symptoms right out of your body.

Your body may very well look like you have a cold. Your nose may be runny, and you may be coughing frequently. Your co-workers may come up to you and ask if you are catching a cold. Nevertheless, you must make sure that your confession agrees with the Word of God. Instead of saying, "Well, I guess I am coming down with a cold," say, "I believe that I am healed."

Treat symptoms like a package someone delivers to your home, and they have the wrong address. When they ask you to sign for the package, refuse to do it. Refuse to accept it. That is the way you have to treat sickness when it attacks your body. The package of sickness comes from Satan. When it comes knocking at your door, he has the wrong address because sickness does not belong to you; therefore, do not sign for the package. The way you sign for the package is by your confession. One way you sign for the package is by saying, "I am sick."

When symptoms of sickness first attack your body, deal with it immediately. When the first sign of a symptom comes, no matter how small it may be—it may be a sore throat or a cough—bombard those symptoms with the Word of God.

> Ephesians 6:13, 14
> 13 Therefore take up the whole armor of God, that you may be able to withstand in the evil day, and HAVING DONE ALL, TO STAND.
> 14 STAND THEREFORE, having girded your waist with truth, having put on the breastplate of righteousness (Emphasis added)

Stand firm against the attack and refuse to be moved from your position of faith. Immediately, jump on those symptoms by speaking the Word against them. Here is an example of how to resist the devil's attack. Say, "No you don't devil. You are not going to put this sickness on me because 1 Peter 2:24 says, 'By whose stripes I was healed.' And Matthew 8:17 says, 'He Himself...bore my sicknesses.'"

> James 4:7
> 7 Therefore submit to God. Resist the devil and he will flee from you.

Resisting sickness is resisting the devil because sickness comes from the devil. To resist means, "to stand firm against." When we stand firm against sickness and disease, it will flee from us.

13.
Healing Confessions

My son, give attention to my words; Incline your ear to my sayings. Do not let them depart from your eyes; Keep them in the midst of your heart;
For they are life to those who find them, And HEALTH TO ALL THEIR FLESH.
—Proverbs 4:20-22 (Emphasis added)

Verse 22 says that the Word is health to all our flesh. The Hebrew word health can also be translated as medicine. The Word of God is medicine to your body, and the best type of medicine is preventative medicine. God's best is not divine healing—God's best is divine health. That is the place where you do not need healing because you are well.

Jesus said in Mark 11:23 that you can have whatever you say. Confessing the scriptures is taking Word medicine. The following are confessions you can make to keep you well.

Father, I thank you that your Word is medicine to all my flesh. I thank you that Jesus Christ took my infirmities and bore my sicknesses and with Jesus' stripes I was healed.

I thank you that no plague shall come nigh my dwelling because I dwell in the secret place of the Most High. I abide under the shadow of the Almighty.

You sent your Word and healed me. You healed all my diseases and delivered me from all my destruction. I have been redeemed from the curse of the law, which is poverty, sickness, and spiritual death. You are the Lord that heals me. You said that you would take sickness out of the midst of me, and the number of my days I shall fulfill.

I declare before heaven and earth and all the demons and imps of hell that I am healed. I will live until I am satisfied with life, for you said in your Word Father that with long life You will satisfy thee and show thee my salvation. In Jesus' Name.

Those confessions are based upon many of the scriptures that we covered in this study. Confessions such as these will strengthen you in your inward man and build up your faith.

Many people think that 1 Peter 2:24 is referring to spiritual healing.

> 1 Peter 2:24
> 24 who Himself bore our sins in His own body on the tree, that we, having died to sins, might live for righteousness—by whose stripes you were healed.

The healing spoken of here cannot be spiritual healing because we are not healed spiritually. When we are born again, we are not healed spiritually—we are made brand new.

> 2 Corinthians 5:17
> 17 Therefore, if anyone is in Christ, he is a new creation...

> Ezekiel 11:19
> 19 Then I will give them one heart, and I will put a new spirit within them...

> Ezekiel 36:26
> 26 "I will give you a new heart and put a new spirit within you; I will take the heart of stone out of your flesh and give you a heart of flesh."

These two passages are clearly prophecies of the new birth experience. Notice that healing is not mentioned because we are not healed spiritually—we are made brand new. The only healing 1 Peter 2:24 could be talking about was physical healing.

> Joshua 1:8
> 8 This Book of the Law shall not depart from your mouth, but you shall meditate in it day and night, that you may observe to do according to all that is written in it. For then you will make your way prosperous, and then you will have good success.

The Book of the Law refers to the first five books of the Bible—Genesis through Deuteronomy. For God's people today, the New Testament saints, the Word of God for us is the Word in light of the finished work of Jesus.

Let us paraphrase the first part of Joshua 1:8 this way, "The word of God shall not depart out of your mouth." In other words, we should speak the Word of God at all times. In this verse, God tells us that one of the ingredients for having good success is to keep speaking the Word of God.

> Proverbs 18:21
> 21 Death and life are in the power of the tongue, And those who love it will eat its fruit.

The Bible says that death and life are in the power of the tongue. With your tongue, you either speak death to your life or life to your life. God's Word is life to those who find them (Proverbs 4:22). The way you speak life to your life is by speaking the Word.

> Hebrews 10:23
> 23 Let us hold fast the confession of our hope without wavering, for He who promised is faithful.

The word *confession* means, "to speak the same thing. So when we confess God's Word, we are speaking the same thing that God says. By doing so, we are agreeing with God. This verse tells us that we should hold fast to our confession or to our speaking the same thing that God says. To hold fast means "to hold on and do not let go." Do not let go. Do not stop saying what God says. Keep on speaking the Word of God and the Word of God will change your life.

> Mark 11:23
> 23 For assuredly, I say to you, whoever says to this mountain, 'Be removed and be cast into the sea,' and does not doubt in his heart, but believes that those things he says will be done, he will have whatever he says.

Jesus said you can have whatever you say if you believe in your heart and do not doubt. If you want to live in divine health, you must learn to speak healing over your body. Notice that Jesus did not say that you would have what you believe. He said that you would have what you say. So you see, it is not enough to believe the Scriptures. You can believe the Scriptures on the subject of healing and still not get healed.

You need to believe the healing Scriptures, but do not stop there. You must speak or confess those healing Scriptures that you believe. You must speak them out of your mouth because Jesus said you would have what you say. Praise God, if you speak healing, you will have healing.

In conclusion, I want to give you some more Bible-based confessions that you can speak over your life. If you make these confessions regularly and believe what you are saying, it will release the healing power of God in your body.

> The Word of God is medicine to all my flesh.
> —Proverbs 4:22

> You sent your word and healed all my diseases and delivered me from all my destructions.
> —Psalm 107:20

> Jesus took my infirmities and bore my sicknesses, and with His stripes I was healed.

—Matthew 8:17 and 1 Peter 2:24

You are the Lord who heals me.
—Exodus 15:26

No plague shall come near my dwelling; therefore, every disease, sickness, germ or virus that touches my body, I bind it and command it to die instantly; and I loose health and healing in my body, in the Name of Jesus.
—Psalm 91:10, John 14:13-14, Matthew 16:19

The law of the Spirit of life in Christ Jesus has made me free from the law of sin and death, sickness and disease.
—Romans 8:2

I am redeemed from the curse of the law; therefore I am redeemed from the curse of sickness.
—Galatians 3:13-14

Healing belongs to me because I am a child of God.
—Luke 13:16

I resist sickness and it flees from me.
—James 4:7

My body is the temple of the Holy Spirit and I glorify God in my body by eating healthy foods   —1 Corinthians 6:19-20

You have taken sickness out of the midst of me. With long life I shall be satisfied. God will bless my bread and my water and the number of my days I will fulfill.
—Psalm 91:16, Exodus 23:25-26

STAY CONNECTED WITH AL

Website: summitministries.tv
Blog: aljennings.com
YouTube: youtube.com/aljennings
Facebook: facebook.com/DrAlJennings
Instagram: draljennings
Twitter: aljennings

Free Daily E-Mail Devotional
Sign up at: http://bit.ly/2unMaNO

ABOUT THE AUTHOR

Dr. Jennings travels throughout the United States and internationally ministering the gospel of Jesus Christ. His purpose is to teach people how to win in life through an understanding of God's unconditional love and grace. He wants people to know that God is a good God and that He's not mad at them; He's madly in love with them.

Dr. Jennings is the author of *Unlocking the Mystery of Tongues, Your Life Matters to God: How to Live Free from Fear in Troubled Times, Basic Training for Victorious Christian Living, God is Not Mad at You; He's Madly in Love with You, Gospel Sketchnotes: A Compilation of Messages by Dr. Al Jennings.*

www.aljennings.com

Made in United States
Troutdale, OR
12/09/2023